SHAWNA J. TALLEY

Hitting the Trail

A guide for those on the path to adulthood and for those preparing them for it.

First edition

Editing by Christie Hagerman
Cover art by Christie Hagerman

This book was professionally typeset on Reedsy.
Find out more at reedsy.com

To Chris, for being the most perfect trailmate that God could have chosen for me.
To Sam, Katelyn, Zane, and Evan, for being my life's greatest adventure. I cannot wait to see where God takes you in your own paths.
To my Coyotes, for being my inspiration, encouragement, and barista family.
And to Christie, for being my Sherpa in the truest sense.

Contents

Preface

I never thought I'd be here. I am an old soul. When I was in my teen and early adult years, my mind and soul were years beyond my age. For this reason I rarely had relationships with my peers. I sought out older friends and found my home with those who were in much different stages than I was. So it came as a great surprise when God plopped me right into the middle of a shop full of just the ones who I had spent a lifetime avoiding. Let me tell you how….

In the summer of 2015 we were faced with a minor financial crisis that required that I head back into the workforce part-time. I had worked odd jobs for years, but this was the first time that I actually left my children at home to work a job. The options of where I could work were limited, in that I had a 4-year-old and was homeschooling our other three children, ages 9, 11, and 14. The only available time that I could find to work was the time that was spent sleeping, so I began searching for businesses that opened very early with a morning rush hour that might benefit from an extra hand. After a multitude of calls, I finally landed on a small, locally-owned coffee shop that was willing to give me a chance.

Needless to say, after 15 years of being my own boss, and coming from a position of high management at a large non-profit agency, pouring coffee and taking orders from high school students was humbling at best. Waking up pre-dawn each day and trudging to a job that was menial in comparison to my past positions took more grit than I was sure this tired mama of four could muster. Add to this a strained work environment, and I more than questioned why God had placed me here. However, eight months in, His intentions became very clear. While most of my co-workers ranged in age from 17-25, they all seemed to be in a similar stage of life. Some had a very clear direction for their lives, but many of my young friends candidly shared feelings of anxiety and apprehension as they ventured into adulthood.

As relationships strengthened, I enjoyed sharing experiences and guidance with some of the girls. Soon they began to share with me many of the concerns and uncertainties of their lives. Having an encouraging spirit, I was excited for God to use my gift in the oddest of places. The girls at the shop became like daughters to me. I found that God often laid them on my heart for prayer and encouragement. He led me in sensing when they needed someone to talk to and often audibly urged me to reach out to one girl or another. Young ladies came and went at the shop, but there was always at least one or two that I connected to and who grabbed hold of my heart. It was then that I realized that my minor financial crisis had very little to do with my finances. God had a very specific purpose for me to be pouring coffee and blending frappes. He began to use me in a way that I never could have imagined, yet that I was so very grateful for.

My life has been richer since the day I began to work at the coffee shop, and not simply financially. The relationships I have formed and the blessings I have received have been nothing short of Providential. The lessons have gone beyond just relationships. God has used every minute of my time there to remind me of the struggles of young adults and the challenges that they face in this tumultuous time. My thumb was so off of the pulse of what this generation is going through; walking through life with these young adults has allowed me to gain knowledge that has been invaluable in raising my own children into adulthood. And yet, God was quick to remind me that this knowledge did not need to stop at my own children. My heart has overflowed with the joy of working with amazing young people. They have inspired me daily to revisit my journey through the past 25 years and to dig deep to find the lessons and wisdom that God so richly poured into me. Needless to say, I have gained much more than any one of my fellow baristas.

My prayer for you, my dear Reader, is to realize that our life is but a journey and we are all walking our unique paths. Whether you are just beginning your path into adulthood, you are an adult who has lost your way, or you are a parent ushering your child onto their own path, may the words of these pages bring you encouragement, courage, resources, and fortitude for the journey. God makes no mistakes as to where you are in your journey and where you are going. My life is a living picture of the surprising and glorious places He will take you when you trust every step to Him!

This is not a book to sit back and enjoy, but to strap on a backpack and tie on a good pair of boots. We have an exhilarating adventure to begin!

I

Our Journey

1

The Path - God's Plan

My feet have closely followed His steps; I have kept to His way without turning aside. Job 23:11[1]

I love to hike. I love the adventure. The unknown. The challenges. The scenery. The topography. Everything about choosing a desired destination, preparing for the journey, studying the maps, consulting the field guides, and hitting the trail. There is a thrill in what I will experience, and a bit of an adrenaline rush from the unknown challenges ahead. Every trail, every destination, and every adventure have the same thing in common for me: the security that my journey will be just that, mine. No other hiker will have the same experience. No other traveler will see what I see. The trail, the weather, the scenery, and the topography, are ever-changing, and my experience will be unique to me. No one will ever recreate it. The people I encounter, the challenges I face, the creatures that will cross my path will never impact anyone else in the same way. Ever.

Life is such a journey. It is full of the thrill of new experiences and the adrenaline rush of unknown challenges. It comes with its own scenery, topography, weather, creatures, and fellow travelers. It is ever-changing. And it is unique to each of us. Our journey is just that, ours. No one can recreate it. No one will have the same encounters and challenges that we have. Our destination, however, is hopefully the same: life eternal with God in heaven. Not everyone will choose this destination, and we will discuss this in a later chapter. But for now, my prayer is that we all have our eyes on the same goal, and this book will be based on the premise that our journey will lead us to this glorious Ultimate Destination. So let us dive into what we will find on this journey and begin our adventure together

Other than your destination, the most important decision to make when beginning an adventure is choosing which path you will take to get there. As I have experienced every time I've stepped foot on a trail, I have to choose a path. The options are often numerous; regardless, I have to pick. It is most likely the hardest choice I make throughout the entire journey. It defines my direction, and sets the stage for the entire experience. It is a critical step that must take place before my feet even hit the dirt. It will determine my success or failure in my journey. With this choice comes an acceptance of everything I will encounter from that point forward. It is my journey. And you have a journey too. Let's lace up our boots, grab our hiking stick, and see what lies ahead!

Which Way?

In our life, we will all have to decide a path. Not one person is exempt from this decision. The path we choose will define who we are, the decisions we will make, and the direction we will take. Life will offer many options in how we travel, where we go, and who we meet, but the path we set ourselves upon lays the foundation for these variables. Each of us has our own path, unique to ourselves. No other person can walk this path for us, for God designed it uniquely for our life and His goals for our life. The path that God intends for us is distinctly designed with our strengths, talents, gifts, and abilities in mind. God does not make mistakes when He sets our path before us. He knows exactly what lies ahead, and thus equips us accordingly. He sees our entire path and gives us what we need to tackle the terrain, weather, obstacles and encounters with others that we cannot see with our human eyes.

When we choose a path that is grounded in God, it is like a train on a track that proceeds easily along to its destination, having full confidence that the track will keep it moving along the right path. It is for this reason that it is wise for a person to set themselves upon the path that God intends for us. In Psalm 37:23 the psalmist declares this truth: "You [God] will make known to me the path of life; you will fill me with joy in your presence, with eternal pleasures at your right hand."

Once this decision is made, I cannot guarantee that the journey will be any easier, but I can guarantee that we will find assurance in our direction that will bring continued peace and contentment, no matter what we encounter. Keeping our eyes focused on God's direction will allow us to take in the scenery and experience life in its fullness because we will not have to continually stop to check our coordinates.

Navigational Tools

My mother raised me to love navigating. When we took trips, I would sit in the passenger seat, maps sprawled across my lap, and direct her around every turn. It was hard work. I was constantly checking where we were against where we needed to be going. I couldn't take my eyes off of the route or we would end up lost. I loved this job but missed a lot of the scenery because I had my head in the maps. Then the GPS was invented (I know, I'm dating myself here!) This is a magnificent creation. Now I can put my destination into the device and sit back and relax while my personal electronic guide tells me exactly where to go. I don't have to do nearly as much work or be quite as concerned about getting lost. And I get to look up and take in the exciting places and experiences around me!

Think of God as your personal GPS. Let's call it our God's Positioning System. God has already plugged in our destination and all we have to do is sit back and listen to His voice to direct us. Once we do this, we can get our head out of the maps and enjoy the experiences around us. Living without our GPS requires us having to navigate life on our own. It means burying ourselves in the maps and guides and being in a constant state of concern for getting lost. It means missing out on life around us because we are so focused on our own route. And when we are spending all of our energy trying to navigate our own path, we most certainly will not have the energy to see what is going on with those around us. We may bypass many amazing views because we have our heads in the maps that the world has to offer. Believe me, Fellow Traveler, those maps are always lacking. Many travelers won't even be able to find their starting point. They don't know where they are or where to begin.

At this very time in your life, you need to make a decision as to what path you are on. Are you going to let God set your destination and then tune in to His voice to guide you? If so, you need to make a conscious decision daily to listen to the Spirit of God and allow Him to direct you. This decision will not be easy; just as I have to make a choice to turn on my GPS and trust it to bring me to my destination, so must we make a daily choice to tune into our Heavenly Father and trust that He will bring us to our Ultimate Destination. It takes a conscious surrender of your plans to His will. My prayers are that through this book you will choose to follow the One True Path to the most spectacular destination you could ever imagine.

Deviating from the Trail

Sadly, I know that many will not make this decision. Maybe you have not. Maybe you believe that you are the most capable to navigate your journey. Maybe you intended to follow God's path, but you got distracted and deviated from your trail. Maybe you saw a better view or an easier path and chose to take that instead. Maybe the terrain seemed smoother, simpler to navigate. Maybe the people on a different path seemed to be having a much better time. All of these thoughts can convince us that the path that God set for us is not for us. It is during these times of desiring to depart from our intended path that we become disoriented. We choose a different route and are often not prepared to face what that journey will entail.

This may be where you are today, Friend. This may be where you have been in the past, or a place you will be facing soon. Before you take another step in the wrong direction, let us take a look at some possible consequences of leaving the secure path that God has placed us on in order to navigate a different trail:

1. *We become lost.* I will admit to you that through our many years of hiking as a family, I have had a few times when I decided for one reason or another not to follow the designated path. Sometimes that is due to my lack of understanding of the trail map, my failure to look at a map, or my desire to find a more enjoyable route. Whatever the reason, I somehow managed to get my family lost. Being lost is simply not fun. Oftentimes when we have been lost, we have ended up walking many miles out of our way, which was miserable because we were already hot, tired, and frustrated. As the one responsible for my family's safety, being lost can be a frightening experience. It causes anxiety and feelings of hopelessness. Those times when I led my crew astray, I had to face the reality that I was most definitely not in control, and that I was at the mercy of the woods. I felt inadequate and helpless. Have you ever been in a place of feeling lost? It is not a comfortable place to be, is it? It is scary and unsettling, and most definitely not where we want to stay for very long. Choosing to navigate life on our own leaves us susceptible to losing our way. It is a risk that we must assume; even when the result may be unfavorable.

2. *The trail is much more difficult.* My eldest son is an adventurer through and through. He loves being in the woods, even more than I do, and truly loves to blaze his own trail. From a young boy, he would jump at every chance he had to deviate from the trail to a more challenging route while we were hiking. From climbing steep cliffs to balancing on fallen trees over treacherous ravines to sloshing through creeks and streams, he always longed to take the more interesting path. Those challenges were enticing to him. As a mom, I teetered on the fence of adventure versus danger. Most of the time my adventurous spirit gave in and I let him forge his own trail. Although he always made it to the desired location, it was a difficult path. He put forth much more effort than the rest of us. He would often come out wet, scratched, sweaty, and out of breath. For a young boy, putting forth more effort on a small hike is not a big deal; however, for an adult on

a lifelong journey, taking the hard way can become exhausting. You will run out of energy and weary quickly of expending the extra effort. You may come out worn and tattered. It is crucial for us to know the possible consequences of choosing the more difficult route. Are we prepared to accept what we might encounter when we stray from the intended path? That is a question, Dear Traveler, that we must answer for ourselves.

3. *We are not prepared for the journey.* God has equipped us perfectly for the journey that He intends for us. He gives us the exact gifts, abilities, and tools we need for anything we will encounter. When we choose to travel a different path, we cannot be guaranteed that we will possess what we need. For example, it would be foolish of me to take a hike in the snowy mountains if all I had with me was a swimsuit and sunscreen. They wouldn't do me much good, would they? Now, that may sound preposterous, yet how often do we get ourselves into situations that we are not prepared for? We lack the necessary resources and then question why we fail. We get mad at God or those around us, and blame them for our failure. In reality, we need to assess whether we are where we are supposed to be. Are we on the right path? If we have left the trail God prepared us for, we are susceptible to failure or possible pain. God is exact in His preparations for us, but when we refuse to stay on His path, we forfeit the benefit of those preparations. If I disregard the comfort and security of a warm coat and hat and choose to tackle the mountain in my bikini, I must be prepared to accept the frostbite that ensues. Preparation is a key to success; why not allow the Master Packer to ensure your victory?

4. *We meet unfriendly travelers.* At any given time, our lives are intersecting with other people. When we are on our intended path, God has ordained those intersections to enhance our journey. We may meet someone who will guide us, someone who will encourage us, someone who will thrill us. If we veer from our path, we may

inherently come into contact with unfriendly travelers. What does this mean? Satan is very good at using our deviance from God as an easy opportunity to bring unhealthy influences into our lives. That may come in the form of meeting people who will entice us into doing things we normally wouldn't do and thinking ways we typically wouldn't think. Satan will use anything he can to bring destruction into our lives.

I am reminded of the story of *Beauty and the Beast*. When Belle's father, Maurice, finds himself lost in the woods in the middle of the night, he chooses the wrong path, which leads him face to face with the terrifying beast. This encounter begins a series of unfortunate events that leads to pain and destruction for himself, his daughter, the beast, and several others in the town.

Although we realize that this is a fictional story, it can serve as a vivid illustration to the path of destruction that can follow us when we become lost and choose the wrong path. Satan is waiting for us to step off of our safe and God-protected path and onto the unfamiliar path that will leave us vulnerable to his attacks. It is the quintessential dilemma of being in the wrong place with the wrong people at the wrong time. Satan is waiting to intersect your path with unfriendly travelers who would love nothing more than to kill, steal, and destroy you in your journey.

Disclaimer: Although stepping from the path leaves us susceptible to Satan's advances, I need to clarify here that sometimes bad things happen even when we are strictly following God's direction. All man has free will, and we are all vulnerable to the effects of that.

5. *We end up further from our destination.* Have you ever thought that you would take a short-cut, and you actually ended up much further from where you wanted to go? I love to test my navigating skills and

often try a new route - against the advice of my GPS - to see if I can find a better way to reach our location. This rarely works out and I end up getting turned around, disoriented, and far from where I intended to be. When we try to take a short-cut or better route through life - against the advisement of God - we will most likely face the same fate. In our effort to do things our way, we become turned around, disoriented, and far from where God intends for us to be.

This may come in the form of being dishonest at work to gain a promotion, being unfaithful to a friend or significant other to indulge our own desires, or being prideful to advance ourselves to where we believe we ought to be. Don't get me wrong - there is nothing wrong with wanting to succeed in life. However, when we seek out success by taking the seemingly easy route, we may be purposely or inadvertently circumnavigating God's path for a more appealing one. While these deviations in our route may seem to be taking us on a quicker path to our desired destination, we often find that we end up much farther away from where God ordained for us to be.

After assessing where the wrong path can lead us, is it any wonder that so many find life to be so grueling? Following Christ through life does not mean that our path will be smooth and sunny; it will still bring with it hardships and fear and stormy weather. How we travel our path and our ability to handle those hardships are what will set our journey apart from the ones traveling without guidance. We will discuss this more in a later chapter, but for now, let's turn up our volume on our GPS and make preparations for our journey.

Travel Notes:

Have you ever been physically lost? Write down the feelings that you encountered during that time.

In your life journey, have you had times when you've encountered these same feelings? If so, when?

Have you ever used a GPS while traveling? What benefit did it offer to you?

What has influenced your life direction up to this point? Has it prevented you or encouraged you to listen to your God's Positional System?

What possible benefits do you see you can gain from using your God's Positioning System? What changes can you make to tune into Him more?

2

Getting to the Summit - Eternal Destination

For God so loved the world that He gave His one and only Son,
so that whoever believes in Him shall not perish but have eternal life. John
3:16[2]

As we go through life, we have two choices: to follow God's path for our life or to attempt the journey on our own, both in hopes that we will reach our desired destination. Each choice comes with its own set of risks. Placing our life in the hands of the unseen takes a great deal of faith. We may not have the reassurance of having control over our path. For many, this is terrifying, and understandably so. On the contrary, placing our life in our own hands takes a great deal of assumed self-reliance. The truth is, we do not have the ability to control our path. This is also a terrifying thought, but for far greater reasons. We are not wired to see our future. If we were, one can only imagine the mess we would make trying to get there.

Have you ever been shopping on Black Friday? Herds of people cramming into stores to gain the newest "hot deal" of the season. They push, trample, and crawl their way into the store, and then wait in lines for hours to purchase their treasures. I sometimes envision this as what would happen if we were able to see into our future. Would we push, trample, and claw our way up to attain our desired treasure? Satan has promised us a "hot deal" if we just do things our way. In the end, I would venture to say that we will find that the process and the product fall significantly short of what we desired.

God uniquely designed His plan so that our time on this earth is a mystery. One thing I have been reminded of through raising teens is that they are extremely confident and optimistic about their future. They plan when they will marry, how many children they will have, what their house will look like. They are not wrong in wanting to make a plan. It is encouraging to see them investing time and effort into their dreams. But there is an element of reality that they lack. It is very simple to pick a spouse, kids, house, and career from the comfort of a teenage bedroom, unjaded by life experiences. The reality is that not one of us has the ability to plan out every piece of our future. Life changes by the minute, and an unrealistic hope in what we cannot control can be misleading to a young person.

If you are a young adult, it is important to have a dream; however, self-reliance in achieving that dream can be destructive. The truth is that the future is unknown. Just as I have no ability to change the topography of the trail that I am hiking, there is not one person on this earth that can control the path to their future, despite what Satan would have us believe. He loves to convince us that we call the shots, that we can choose what happens to us. In a way we can, but not in the way many people would imagine. God gave His children free will. We have the ability to make choices about life, and these choices do affect outcome.

We also have the ability to influence the journey as we go our own way. In a worldly sense, this may be ideal. Yet this sense of control is an illusion because in a worldly sense, what we hope to accomplish on our journey is skewed. We are told by Satan and by the world that what we ought to desire is comfort, convenience, prosperity, fortune. That our way is the best way to get what we want. That our autonomous path will lead to the best views.

Yet God tells us that we ought to desire eternal life with Him, because the world will disappoint us. Jesus reassures us in John 16:33, "I have told you these things so that in me you may have peace. In this world, you will have trouble. But take heart! I have overcome the world." Satan persuades us that on our own, we will find prosperity and wealth. Jesus tells us directly that this world will bring with it hardship and pain. Do you see the discord between what Satan would have us to believe and what God promises for us?

Such a comforting and popular verse that we see often is Jeremiah 29:11. If this is familiar to you, please do not skim over the words. Let them permeate you for a moment. See them as if for the first

15

time. "'For I know the plans I have for you,' declares the Lord, 'plans to prosper you and not to harm you, plans to give you hope and a future.'" For He knows the plans *He* has for you. Our Father has taken the love and care to lay out a plan for your life since before you were conceived. And according to the prophet Jeremiah, the Lord never intends harm for us. Never. He offers us a direct route to Him. We will most definitely face hardship. He does not promise us that our path will be easy. But He knows that when we put our faith in Jesus the destination is assured and will never change.

All Paths Do Not Lead Home

A popular question that many people struggle with is whether there truly is only one way to everlasting life with God in Heaven. Dr. Keith Shorter, Senior Pastor at Mt. Airy Baptist Church, preached a sermon concerning the ways to eternal life, in which he addressed that there is a growing belief that there are many ways to get to heaven, and all we have to do is choose which one we like best.[3]

According to a study conducted by the Barna Group, "Millenials are less likely to believe that Jesus is the path to Heaven than are other generations." The study indicates that less than half of millennials believe that Jesus was God (48%), and 35% say Jesus was merely a spiritual leader.[4] As Dr. Shorter explains, universalism tells us that there are multiple ways to get to God and that all paths lead to the summit of God. Yet in John 14:6 Jesus tells his disciples, "I am the way, the truth, and the light. No one comes to the Father except through me." According to Dr. Shorter,

Jesus is the only way to God. Not one way or a better way, but THE WAY. Jesus loved us enough to come to earth and point us to exactly the path we need to take to get to God. He escorts us personally to the Father.

Acts 4:12 reveals that "salvation is found through no one else, for there is no other name under heaven given to mankind by which we must be saved."

The verse in John verifies some basic questions that we all have grappled with: How can I get to heaven? How can I be sure of that? How can I be satisfied with my life? Dr. Shorter tells that John 14 answers these questions quite directly: Jesus is the Way, we can be sure because He is the Truth, and we can be satisfied because He is the Life!

What assurance we find in knowing that if we maintain our course on the One True Path of God, through the guidance of Jesus and the Holy Spirit, our destination is eternal life with Him in Heaven. And this path that God offers us to Him is not exclusive. "It is not a narrow path, it is wide enough to include every man on earth. We don't need multiple ways to God, we just need to be thankful that there is a Way" (Shorter). Jesus gives us this path through His death on the cross, and God provided that Way by sacrificing His only son for us.

Our specific journey may be an unknown, but our path does not have to be. Although we will not always see what lies ahead, we can find assurance that when we are following Jesus we can rest in confidence in the path. Experiencing eternal life in the presence of our Heavenly King is what God so desperately desires for all of His children. He allows every individual to choose the path that leads to Him.

Friend, do not be fooled by the world into thinking that you can control your destiny. God longs for each of us to choose His Way, in order that we may enjoy the riches of His Kingdom. Allow yourself to trust each step to Him. Making the choice to enter His path will be the most important decision you will make in your life. Again, He does not promise this path to be easy, but He does promise that His

Destination will be worth every step!

Travel Notes:

Are you prone to desire control over your life? Circle a number on the Control-o-Meter that describes how much:
(less) 1 2 3 4 5 6 7 8 9 10 (more)

List some dreams you have for your life - these may include relationships, career, living situations, education, etc.

Of the above list, circle which ones you feel you have total control over?

What in your life can bring you assurance of the future?

Have you sought eternal assurance from God, the only One who can fulfill promises for your future? If not, I urge you to speak to someone about how to commit your life to God through salvation found in Jesus Christ.

3

Clipping In - Faith in Action

The LORD is good, a refuge in times of trouble. He cares for those who trust in him. Nahum 1:7[5]

Any avid hiker will agree that one of the most valuable assets on a treacherous trail is a guide rope. These are ropes or cords that are anchored to the side of a mountain or ravine, which allow the hiker to clip his/her carabiner on for added safety. It is in the act of clipping that the hiker places full trust in the rope for his/her safety and success.

The sections of a trail that typically warrant these aids are the ones that are the most uncertain: a steep incline, a narrow trail, a muddy or slippery passage, a wide ravine, a makeshift bridge. It is here where the hiker will require assistance in order to successfully navigate the obstacle. These areas can be scary to the most experienced hiker. They are challenging and require a great amount of courage to tackle.

Similarly, there are times in our lives where we face uncertain circumstances: the loss of a loved one, job insecurity, financial stress, physical or mental illness, or many more possibilities. These times in our lives are scary and will require us to seek assistance to navigate them. Luckily for us, God provides us with a Guide Rope on His path as well. He sent Jesus, His son, to be our Ultimate Guide Rope. And the most amazing thing about God is that He provides assistance not only in the treacherous times of our lives, but at all times.

When I think of Jesus, I immediately think of two words: *relationship* and *connection*. The purpose for Jesus taking on human form and coming to this earth was so that we can understand and form a relationship with our Creator God, and to allow us access to God. When I think of Jesus, I envision Him from the stories of the Bible. I am able to put a face to a name. I think of Him as a tangible person, someone I can touch and feel. When we form a relationship with someone, we feel them, maybe not always physically, but emotionally. My favorite quality of Jesus is that in Him coming to us, He brought me the opportunity to feel God. I feel a connection to God through Jesus that I do not think would have been possible if He had not become man.

I have always thought of Jesus as not only my friend, but also my guide. He is the same for all of us. Jesus can be counted as our friend, in that

He is always here for us, and I believe that He longs to have the same relationship with us that He had with His disciples. When we study the New Testament we can see how much He loved those around Him, and how much He desired to teach them and guide them toward a relationship with Him and with God the Father.

This is the Jesus that is accessible for all of us. And this is the Jesus who longs to be our Guide Rope. He came to earth specifically to show us the way to have a relationship and connection with our Father God, so it only makes sense that He is there at all times in our lives to ensure that we have access to do the same.

It is important that we clip into this amazing Guide. It is Jesus who will keep us on the right path to God, especially in the times when life tries to disorient us with treacherous conditions. These times in our lives are challenging and scary, and will take great strength and courage to clip into Jesus and trust in the security of His love.

When We Don't Want to Clip In

Although having Jesus as our Guide Rope is a trustworthy source of security, there undoubtedly will be times when we feel we don't need His assistance. We feel we can handle all that life is giving us. We become autonomous on our path and determined to travel it alone. Let us look for some possible reasons for this:

We will feel that life is going well and we do not need His help. Oftentimes, when life seems to be good and things are all falling into place, we diminish our need for God. And even more so, we fail to recognize the role that He has played in getting us there. We become surefooted and convinced that we are responsible for the good things that are happening in our life. Our successes become a source of pride and we swell with confidence in our abilities. In and of itself, being proud

21

of what we accomplish is not sinful. It is good to have confidence. Where the sin creeps in is when we become fooled into thinking that we are *the reason* for our prosperity.

It is important to remember Who directs our paths, and Who is responsible for our success in our journey thus far. God loves to see His children thrive! He loves to provide us great scenery and a leisurely path through life. A hiker who experiences easy paths and wide clearings would be easily fooled into believing that they are an expert explorer. Just as easily can we be convinced that we are an expert in the Game of Life. Whereas God provides us a smooth trail at times that He desires to give us rest and refreshment, I believe Satan can use this time to convince us that we can do anything and that we do not need God anymore. With this in mind, we need to step back in times of prosperity – not just financial, but spiritual, physical, and emotional prosperity as well – and ask God to use it as a way to build our confidence in Him more than in ourselves. It is important for us to gain independence and confidence in our abilities to tackle life's path. However, an inflated image of our abilities can rob us from learning crucial lessons that will help us to navigate the path when it isn't so serene.

We are ashamed to admit that we need His help. In rough times, it is easy to fail to ask for guidance from anyone. Again, pride seeps in and we become afraid to ask for help, or we feel that we have what it takes to handle it by ourselves. When times are tough – we are frustrated or feeling defeated – it is common to turn away from God and refuse to clip in to our Guide Rope. We oftentimes will blame God for our hard times, and feel resentment towards Him. It is very difficult to ask for help from anyone whom we resent. However, these are the times that we need His guidance the most. So many times I have heard people state that it is easy to follow God in the good times, but not so easy in the hard ones. We are quick to have faith in Him when our path is smooth. Not so easy when it becomes scary or questionable.

My family loves to go on trips. We love to travel to new destinations and see things we've never seen before. And I seem to be the ringleader of said adventures most of the time. When the trip is going well – we are easily finding destinations, having fun, and sharing good experiences – my family has faith in me and they willingly put their plans in my hands. But…when the trip does not go so well – we get lost, we are tired and uncomfortable, and our experiences are less than fun – my family slowly begins to question whether they want me as their guide. Their faith in me dwindles with every turn and destination. Their excitement and desire for an adventure fades fast. It just isn't fun anymore and I become the reason for that.

Oftentimes, we do the same to God. When we are having fun in life and enjoying the adventure, we are quick to put our faith in Him. Why wouldn't we? He is taking us great places. But as soon as our trip takes some unpleasant turns, we start to look for someone to blame for our misfortune and quickly lose trust in the One who is our guide. We question whether He really knows the plan and can lead us effectively.

Do you know that something funny happens by the end of my family's crazy, misled adventures? We come away from the trip with a new appreciation for where we've been, what we've been through, and who has taken us there. We always take away a lesson, be it a better way to navigate, communicate, or prepare. We learn new things about each other. And my children always express thanks to me for giving them a unique experience, as strange as it may have been.

Typically, on our way home, I ask each child to share their favorite part of the trip. Their answers always surprise me. And more often than not, their favorite experiences were the hardest parts of the day for me. They were the times that I had to work very hard to pull things together to keep us from becoming completely discouraged and lost. My efforts in guiding my children through those times have never come up void. I have seen growth in all of us with each trial. I see them trust me more with each adventure, because they see me navigating in the thick with them, never giving up trying to make it a memorable experience, and working hard to bring beauty out of the mess of our unfortunate turns.

It makes me wonder if our favorite experiences through our trials may be the hardest part of the journey for God. I cannot imagine what He goes through to lay the guide rope for us to cling to. Who knows what He is doing to provide us a memorable experience amidst our hard times. Just as I desire to ensure my children have a great experience even when things do not go our way, God so much more desires that for *His* children – for us. And He also longs to see our growth through each trial. The desired outcome would be for us to trust Him more, to see that He is in the thick with us, navigating us through and working hard to bring beauty out of our unfortunate turns.

Once Clipped In, Keep Moving

Now that we have established that clipping into Jesus is a necessary step to successfully reaching the ultimate goal of eternal life with Him, we need to address the benefit of staying clipped in. Inevitably, you will experience rough terrain, storms, loose footings, ravines, boulders, and more dangers through your life. It is at these times that being clipped into Jesus will keep you moving in the right direction regardless of your obstacles.

There will be times when you cannot see two feet in front of you, and you are not sure you can take another step. You will live day by day, sometimes minute by minute, because of what life has thrown at you. You may be in this place now. These times bring with them feelings of hopelessness, panic, anxiety, and despair. It is now that you must rely upon the security of that carabiner! Test its strength, grab hold of that rope, and keep pulling yourself forward, one unsure step after another. The winds may blow, the rain may beat down on you, the cliff may be steep, the boulder high, but as long as you keep moving, Jesus will keep guiding you. You have to do your part by moving forward! You can't cross a river by staring at the other side. You have to eventually take a step of faith. When we keep moving through hardship, each step forward is a step of faith. We are trusting that God has a plan, a path, and protection for us.

We had a very long season of storms with one of my children. We often described it as living in the midst of a tornado. Each day we figuratively had to force ourselves to put one foot in front of the other. There were times that we thought we would just get swept up in the winds. It was terrifying, stressful, and seemingly hopeless. But we stayed clipped in to Him. Through the rains and wind, we leaned into Him, depending on His guidance for every step. We crawled, hand-over-hand, along our Guide Rope. We stayed His course.

Now on the other side of the storm, I can say that without staying clipped in, we would have faced complete destruction as a family. The storm would have caused irreparable damage. I do not want to imagine what path our family would have ended up on. Yet He led us to a place of victory. The health professional who treated my child commented that she could not believe that we were able to find healing without certain aids. We worked hard through God to get our child to that point. It was exhausting to pull ourselves through that, but God not only blessed us with a successful outcome, He was able to show my family and an unbelieving professional, the power of faith in Him and of fortitude in weathering the storms with Him. Young Person, clip in. He knows your path. Keep putting one foot in front of the other. God has this, now it is time to put your faith into action.

Trail Guides

We also have another aid that is crucial in our travels. When I am hiking, I may not know where the trail will lead or what I will encounter, but as long as I stay on my path, I find a confidence in the work of the trail guides. The Bible is our life Trail Guide. It leaves us explicit directions of where to find Jesus and how to access His Way. We need to consult it regularly.

The times that I have been lost on a hike are the ones in which I failed to do my research, to consult my guides. I go in blindly and suffer the consequences. During my misguided hikes I regret that I did not take advantage of the resources available to me. I have made the same mistakes in life. The times I am lost and seem to be going in circles are the times I have failed to consult my guide, the Bible. I have wandered blindly through a situation and oftentimes have suffered great consequences in the process. I failed to take advantage of the resources God has given me.

Do not underestimate the power of God's Word. No matter the situation in your life, the Bible has relevance, and it is packed full of directions for living. Seeking out His Word can be intimidating, especially if it is not a common practice for you. May I suggest that the more you are able to consult His Word, heightened understanding will come through familiarity. I found with my hiking guides that it took exploring a few of the hikes in the books for me to become familiar with the benefit of the guide. Until I put my foot to the trail it was difficult to understand its verbiage. In the same way, until we actually put what the Bible tells us into practice in our lives, it is difficult to understand. Simply reading a verse will not gain us understanding into God's direction for us. It is putting what He says into practice that will give us confidence in His Word, just as finding success in my hikes helped me to gain confidence in my trail guides.

When we do this in those tough passages of trail when we are clipped into Jesus as our Guide Rope, we are assured that we are headed in the right direction. It takes faith on our part. We have to trust in those who know what lies ahead of us, who have gone before and scouted out the dangers of the terrain, who have mapped out the path for our greatest experience – with just the right mix of comforts, enjoyment, challenges, and spectacular sights! This is what God longs for. He not only has efficiently equipped us, effectively laid the Guide Rope for us, and explicitly written our Trail Guide, He desires that we seek and trust Him so that we can successfully access life with Him. Clipping into Him is faith in action.

Travel Notes:

Describe a time when you experienced an easy, scenic path through life.

How would you describe your relationship with Jesus during those good times?

Describe a time in your life when you have experienced hard times or uncertain circumstances.

What was your relationship with Jesus during these times?

How can clipping into Jesus affect your personal journey?

HITTING THE TRAIL

4

Backpacks - Gifts and Talents

For we are God's handiwork, created in Christ Jesus to do good works, which God prepared in advance for us to do. Ephesians 2:10[6]

As any wise and competent hiker will tell you, what you carry with you on your journey is the key to your failure or success. A hiker equipped with the right tools will have the confidence to conquer any obstacle along the way. We also have a well-equipped backpack for our metaphorical journey of life. This pack, full of tools and resources, has been packed with care by the Ultimate Hiking Expert, God Himself. He knows exactly what we will each need for our specific journey. Just as a hiker on Mt Everest needs completely different items than the one who is conquering the caverns of Mammoth Cave, each of us has a unique set of tools for exactly the climate and terrain we will experience. And the One who has set our path and who knows what lies ahead is the perfect One to have loaded our backpack for us.

As God reminds us often in His Word, we are unique individuals created by Him:

> *You knit me together in my mother's womb, for you created my inmost being. I will praise Him for I am fearfully and wonderfully made; your works are wonderful, I know that full well. (Psalm 139:13-14)*

> *You know when I sit down and when I rise up; You understand my thought from afar. You scrutinize my path and my lying down, and are intimately acquainted with all my ways. Even before there is a word on my tongue, Behold, O Lord, You know it all. (Psalm 139:2-4 NASB)*

God has given each of us unique gifts and abilities. These gifts and abilities were formed in us at our conception and are the tools and resources that we need to be successful through life. It is essential for us to take inventory of what God has equipped us with before we begin our journey.

30

He created us perfectly. God does not make mistakes. There is not one thing that He placed in us that He cannot use to enhance our experiences. Confidence comes when we can recognize what He has packed for us and we can learn how to use each tool for His glory!

It is important to realize that your pack will look drastically different than everyone else's. What you experience along your path will also look drastically different than others as well. Wisdom comes when we can look at what we have been given and recognize the value that it holds specifically for us. This wisdom often takes years, and possibly decades, to develop. The sooner we are willing and able to take an honest inventory of what tools God has given us, the easier we will navigate our path and the more effective we will be in influencing others through our journey.

Take Inventory

When I was in 8th grade, a mortician visited my school for career day. My entire life I have been enamored with the human body, so this career seemed fascinating to me. I thought that being a funeral home director would be the perfect way for me to meld my love for the human body with my heart to serve others – especially those hurting.

I followed this line of thinking until the next year when my grandmother passed away. Throughout the entire week of visitations with family and friends I used my humor to diffuse the pain of the situation. I told funny antics and cracked jokes about my grandmother. It was then that I realized that my instinct to laugh through a stressful situation may not be the characteristic that would make me the most successful funeral director.

This was one of the first times in my life that I can remember taking a tool inventory. I began to recognize that the tools that God packed for me needed to fit with the direction He was leading me. At this time I realized that there were other career paths that would allow me to use my love of helping others, my interest in biology, and my quirky sense of humor. Who would have thought that these three crazy characteristics could complement each other? Well, God did! This assessment of my gifts led to finding a career in non-profit organizations, where I could laugh and play my way through serving others.

God's creativity never ceases to amaze me. As with any successful plan, knowing our resources is one of the first vital steps we need to take. God does not keep our gifts a secret from us. He longs to see what we can make out of the tools He blesses us with. Satan, on the other hand, wants nothing more than for us to question and doubt what's in our pack. He wants us to think that we don't have what it takes to make it through life. He wants us to search for items that we have no business carrying.

Individual Destinations

I love airports! It thrills me to watch people hustling about in anticipation of new destinations and exciting adventures. When I am packing to travel, I make sure that I have an understanding of where I am going - the climate, the environment, the weather forecast. I assume that most of the other travelers I meet in the airport have done the same. However, what I do not do when I arrive at the airport is compare my luggage to that of the other passengers. See, I do not know what their journey holds.

At any one moment, the very same airport could be a starting point for one traveler, a layover for another, and the final destination for yet another. No one person is there for the same journey. One may be headed to a tropical destination, while another may be facing a wintry wonderland. One may have packed swimsuits, while another long johns. What is in their suitcase is of no concern to me, for I understand that what they need on their journey will be much different than what I will need on mine.

So why is it that we are so concerned for what others possess in their life backpack? They are not on the same journey. Even similar destinations do not have the same route to arrive there. It would not make sense for us to stand at luggage check and question what we have packed based on what the person in front of us has. We do not have knowledge of where they are headed or what they will encounter on the way. In the same way, it does not make sense for us to look at the specific qualities and gifts other people possess and question what God gave us. Our journey is unique and what is required for that journey is unique as well.

Extra Baggage

Our lives are constantly filled with people telling us that we need what others have. Advertisers depend on us believing that we need what they are selling. Social media reminds us that our life looks pathetically different than others. Satan then uses this insecurity to lie to us that what we have isn't enough and what they have is better. He wants to convince us that God failed to sufficiently equip us. If he can get us to question the Creator, then he can get us to question the path and the destination as well. The last thing Satan wants is for us to follow God's path. And he for certain does not want us to reach our God-ordained destination.

The fastest way to hinder our progress and weigh us down in life is to take on items that we don't need. When we insist on carrying baggage that was never intended for us, we take on more than we were meant to bear, which leaves us feeling weary, weak, and worn. God is clear that we do not need what our fellow journeymen carry. "For each of you should use whatever gift you have received to serve others, as graceful stewards of God's grace in its various forms" (1 Peter 4:10 NIV). *In its various forms* indicates that there are many different gifts that God assigns to His believers. The verse does not tell us that we all need to use the same gifts. No, we need to use what *we* received from God. Other travelers will encounter terrain, weather, and obstacles that we may never see, so why would we want to shoulder an extra load that we may never need? It is important that we do not look around at what others have, but keep our focus on the One who knows and provides precisely what our journey requires.

What's in your backpack? There are a multitude of spiritual, physical, and mental gifts that God blesses us with. Recognizing what God has placed in your backpack is crucial in finding confidence and value in your life. No matter what may come into your life, the talents and abilities that God gave you will be enough to get you through it. But the necessity of every tool may not always be clear to you. Sometimes we wonder why God created us with seemingly useless quirks. Again, God does not make mistakes and He uses every bit of what He created in us. Have faith in what your backpack holds. It is packed sufficiently and perfectly for you. Trust in Him as your great Provider and travel on in full confidence of His perfect provisions for His beloved child.

Zip Up Your Pack, Shut Up, and Start Walking

Once you are able to take inventory of all the abilities and talents that God has equipped you with, it is time to start walking. Often in life, I become frustrated and discouraged with my path. I cannot see how I will tackle the current obstacle. I feel defeated. I question my abilities. I question God's provision. I fail to trust Him. During these times, I want to sit down on the side of the road and give up. Or, I want to watch everyone else casually strolling down their path while I moan about how hard my road is. It is at this time that God has a very clear message for me, "Shawna, zip up your pack, shut up, and start walking."

God is quick to remind me in these moments that He has given me all that I need. He admonishes me for my lack of faith and encourages me to trust Him and just keep walking. These are not easy words to swallow, and with my head hung, I slowly rise, sling my pack onto my back, and start walking. It is difficult to put one foot in front of the other. Each step hurts. I do not want to look up because I know the scenery is anything but picturesque. I know what lies ahead may be brutal, painful even. But I also know that He is there. He has prepared the way for me and He has prepared me for the way. "See, I am sending an angel before you to protect you on your journey and lead you safely to the place I have prepared for you" (Matthew 23:20 NLT).

What I need is right beside me. I just need to trust what is in my pack. And the amazing thing about Jesus is this: When we don't even have the strength to look inside the pack for what we need, He is there to hand it to us. He walks beside us, comforting us, encouraging us, and making sure that we have access to all He has packed away for our use on our path. Our flesh often tells us that we are not enough. Satan tells us that we don't have what it takes. The world tells us that we are ill-equipped for its challenges. But God says, "You are enough through Me, you have strength in Me, and you have everything you need from Me; therefore, zip up your pack, shut up, and start walking."

Travel Notes:

Take a good look into your backpack. What gifts and abilities has God packed for you?

What influences do you allow to define how you perceive what is in your backpack?

Is there a trait you feel God has left out, or that you wish you possessed? Ask God to show you the value in the gifts He has blessed you with.

Is it time for you to zip up your pack and start walking? What first steps can you take to trust God more as you tackle the obstacles in your journey?

II

Trail Head

5

On Your Own - Adulthood

You make known to me the path of life; you will fill me with joy in your presence, with eternal pleasures at your right hand. Psalm 16:11[7]

The beginning of any adventure is thrilling. The thrill comes from just that - the start of something new and unknown and the prospect of experiencing that which we have not before. For me and my woods-loving crew, there is nothing more exciting than the sight of a trailhead. Signifying new terrain, scenery, challenges, and the promise of a breathtaking destination, the friendly sign beckons us forward. We are full of anticipation and hope for what lies ahead.

The beginning of adulthood is one of the most recognizable life trailheads we encounter. I also believe it is the one that comes with the most expectation and anxiety. For most young people, a large portion of our lives up to this point have been devoted to thinking, planning, hoping, and dreaming about the future. Then one day, we find ourselves standing at the beginning of the trail - waiting to embark on our very own journey. We are filled with awe at the vast trail as we strain to see what lies ahead. It is a new adventure. Our legs are fresh, our supplies are packed, and we take the first step onto the unfamiliar path. We are headed into unchartered territory and our adventure awaits!

Branching Out

There will come a time in every child's life when it is time to leave the path of their parents or guardians and venture out on their own path. The age this happens is not exact: It may be upper teens or possibly into early twenties. Only the child knows for sure when he or she is ready, which makes for a difficult transition for families. God implants indications in us around this age that it is time to get ready to tackle the trail alone. However, sometimes parents may feel that their child is too young or not ready. To them, the child may seem mentally or spiritually incapable. They may doubt their abilities in the real world. This is why we see so much strife between parents and children around the ages of 16-23. It is here that the rubber meets the road for both parties. As parents, it is a true test of how well we have prepared our children to leave our path and strike it out alone. For children, it is a test of courage – a challenge to overcome feelings of fear and uncertainty, mixed with the excitement and anxiety of beginning a new adventure. So how do we know when it is time?

Discovering What God Put in the Backpack

I think the first step in realizing that a young adult's journey is about to begin is to take a resource inventory. As He has done with every voyager, God has given us each a pack full of resources and gifts. And as we discussed earlier, it is our job to recognize these gifts and to stay in tune with Him enough to know when and how to use the resources He has granted us. Parents need to recognize that children are no different - they also come equipped with a pack of treasures. It is the job of the parent to help their child discover the value in each item and demonstrate for them how and when it is used.

For example, my daughter has a great gift of problem solving. More times than I can count, she has rescued our family with her ingenuity and ability to see and implement solutions. She builds furniture, finds organizational tricks, and invents creative ways to tackle nuisances of a family of six living in a small space. She never ceases to amaze me with her brilliance in this area and others. This resource has proven invaluable to our entire family and I am convinced that this will be one of her strongest abilities as she goes into adulthood. It is my job as her parent to recognize this resource in her, strengthen it by allowing her to use it for the benefit of our family, and teach her how valuable it will be when she is on her own.

Parents need to look closely at their children and assess what gifts God has blessed them with. If the parents cannot recognize them, children will also struggle to do so. Parents need to discover these abilities and make it high priority to ensure that the child can recognize them and knows how to use them. I see many young adults who have no clue what their talents and gifts are, and therefore wander aimlessly through their early adult years feeling useless and lost.

Parents, do not allow your child to leave your path without making sure that they know what God has given them for their journey! If you do not show them, they may never find it. Or worse, they will believe the lies of Satan and others that they don't have anything worthwhile in their pack. It is your job to help them discover how valuable they are. If they do not discover it at this time, their future relationships will struggle because they will not have confidence in what they bring to the journey. They will search for others who have what they feel they lack. However, since God created us to be the completion of what our partner brings, they will find their spouse lacking as well. They will continuously search for someone who has it all, failing to realize that they are actually the one who possesses the needed elements for a successful journey.

In turn, young people, it is your responsibility to look for your gifts before you leave your parent's path. Hopefully, some adult has helped to show you the unique gifts that you possess for this life. Your job is to *believe* them. Then the hardest part begins: trusting in what God has given you. Many young people have parents or mentors who have adequately taught them how to recognize their gifts and how to use them effectively, but once you begin your own journey, it is up to you to look closely at what you are equipped with and remember how to use it.

Our abilities are only as good as our willingness to use them. We cannot go through life blaming others when we fail to use what God has given us. If you are struggling to see your gifts, please find someone who can help you recognize and utilize them: a pastor, friend, mentor, or Christian counselor. It is vital that you know how you are equipped and that you believe that what God has equipped you with is exactly and completely what you will need. Lack of trust in who He has made you to be will cause you to doubt the resources He has given you. This will hold you back in your journey possibly more than any obstacle you will encounter. Young Person, have confidence in yourself! Remember, God made you perfectly for the path He has chosen for you. There is no one else more equipped than you. Trust in Him and His Provision. They will take you far.

If you did not have an adult who has helped you to see what God has given you, then you have to take the initiative to dig deeper into your pack, and to ask God to help you to see. You may not have had good leadership thus far in life, and your journey may have been insecure, uncertain, and possibly downright terrifying. But, Young Person, I want you to have hope! God has not abandoned you, and although you may not have had a strong physical leader to follow, God has been there for every step of your path, and He will continue to be there.

Your path may have been riddled with rocks and mudslides and downed trees that you have had to navigate without the assistance of capable adults, and yet your survival rating has been 100%. You have made it, and those bruises and scratches and scars may not go away, but they are reminders of your strength and your ability in Him to conquer life's toughest obstacles. Though you may be feeling weary and weathered already, your adult journey has just begun. It is essential that you find rest and strength in Him to prepare yourself for what is ahead. He is your refuge. Take time to seek shelter in Him before you go out again. He has a great ability to renew our strength and re-energize us for the coming adventure. You are about to navigate some of the toughest terrain you've seen, so pray up, gear up, and get ready to go!

Rocks vs Resources

As beneficial as my daughter's gift of ingenuity has been, it has also brought with it plenty of obstacles in our path. As we found out through time, and many tears, this gift that we so cherished came hand in hand with diagnoses of dyslexia, dyscalculia, and dysgraphia. For years in our homeschool journey, we crawled through each day, wondering if we would ever reach even the smallest goal. It was rocky, to say the least! Many hours of frustration and failures (on both parties) led to us feeling defeated and helpless. We cried out to God to help us see her gifts amidst the aggravations and misunderstandings.

Then one day, someone sent me a video on dyslexia. In this video, the speaker described characteristics of dyslexic learners and, lo and behold, high mechanical functioning was on the list! One of the strengths of dyslexic learners is a unique ability to see the big picture, which means that their brain can see a problem and visualize the solution. Dyslexic learners often find success in design or mechanical fields because of their gift of creative problem solving. That was my Katie! Oh, how her abilities have been blessings to our family! Though we were often weary from the rocky path that Katie's learning disabilities took us on, the discovery of one of her most valuable strengths was well worth the journey. Isn't it beautiful how God loves to thrill us at the end of a difficult trail with a most precious blessing?

In this same way, you need to use your rocky path to strengthen your resources, not deplete them. What have you encountered that has allowed you to sharpen your skills? Take those moments of uncertainty to look closely at your talents and abilities. You may be pleasantly surprised at what you will find. When we discover the hidden treasures at the bottom of our packs, we can rest in the knowledge that He has fully equipped us, albeit sometimes in the most unexpected ways. Never let your unique qualities hinder your trail progress.

Get Moving!

Recognizing and accepting your gifts and skills will be key to success-fully weathering God's path. As we have discussed before, God wants the very best for His children, but we also have a role in our journey. We were not created to stand still. When you realize that it is your time to begin your own path, you must take action. Choose which path you will follow and then get moving! You cannot begin adulthood without taking the necessary steps. At first you may feel unsure of where you need to go, but with time and with continued reliance and trust in the Father, each step will bring with it more confidence. You will soon discover how well God has prepared you. You will run into fellow travelers who will encourage you along the way. You will gain familiarity with the terrain. All of these things will strengthen you to keep going.

Adulthood is scary. Even those of us who have been on our own path for a long time still encounter sections of trail that disorient us. Do not let fear of the unknown keep you from boldly taking those first steps. Adulthood is inevitable. You cannot remain a child forever. The time for you to make that step will be for you to determine; it is a conscious decision that you will need have the courage to make. Your parents, friends, teachers or family cannot come on your individual journey with you. They will always be there, to mentor and teach you, but these first steps of independence have to come from you. You will know when you are ready, and only then will your personal journey begin.

When my children were young there was always pressure to potty train them. "When did your child become potty trained?" was a common question among moms. It was a pressure put on mothers that was both ridiculous and unnecessary. Despite my best efforts, my child was only going to become potty trained when he was ready. Nothing

I could do would expedite the end result. My typical response to this question was that I was convinced that my son would not go to college in a diaper, so barring that, I was not concerned for when it would happen.

See, he needed to take this necessary step out of babyhood when he was ready. It was solely up to him. I could show him the way to the potty, train him, encourage him, and even put him on a schedule, yet his freedom from diapers was inevitably up to him. Only when he resolved himself to take this step of independence would he successfully leave behind his life of droopy drawers. In the same way, we have to resolve ourselves to enter into adulthood, leaving behind the droopy drawers of childhood and confidently enter into our independent adult journey.

All kidding aside, just as my son was not going to pack his Huggies for college, you are not going to spend the rest of your life clinging to your parent's pant legs. Adulthood comes in time, but ready or not, it does come. A young person is wise to anticipate this transition and take the necessary steps to prepare for it. Just as we had to put effort into preparing my son to use the potty through teaching and encouraging in order to aid in his transition out of diapers, a young person who invests time and energy in seeking out teaching and encouragement will make great strides in ensuring a more successful transition to adulthood.

Finding resources and mentors who have the skills to pass along to you is crucial in finding the confidence for those first steps. Godly mentors, family, church groups for early adults, classes, books, and podcasts from reputable sources are wonderful resources to utilize. However, the absolute best advice that I can give you to prepare you for this new path is to regularly consult your Trail Guide, the Bible. Remember that His word is loaded with trail maps. In its pages He has provided us guidance for every life situation. The knowledge that we have in this extensive aid should calm our fears for our next steps.

For some, adulthood will come at us like a runaway train. For others, it seems to creep at the speed of a hand car on the tracks. Regardless of where you fall on the spectrum, you will stand at the trail head of adulthood one day. It is at this time when you will muster the strength, surety, knowledge, and courage to take your first steps onto your very own path. Yet you will not be alone, so fear not, for "I (God) am with you, each and every day, until the end of the age" (Matthew 28:20 NET).

Travel Notes:

Where are you on your path to adulthood - are you taking those first steps, or have you been on your independent path for awhile?

What are some concerns or obstacles you have encountered as you venture out into adulthood?

Have any of the above caused you to sharpen your skills? If so, how so?

What resources do you have available to you to help you as you begin your new path?

6

Finding Your Footing - Identity

Yet to all who did receive him, to those who believed in his name,
he gave the right to become children of God. John 1:12

In an informal survey of matured (over the age of 30) adults who were asked what they struggled with in early adulthood, there was a resounding commonality - they had trouble finding themselves. What exactly does it mean to *find oneself*? I feel this is an idea that many grapple with because no one truly knows what it means.

First of all, the idea of finding oneself indicates that at some point one has gotten lost. As a child you travel along the path of your parent or guardian. As you grow into adulthood you are beginning to branch off of your parent's path to begin your own. That being said, there are three possible reasons why we may feel as though we are lost from the very start of our path.

1. *You came from an environment of lost-ness.* We have already discussed that up until the point when you enter early adulthood, you have been traveling on the same path as your parents or family. Hopefully, your family has had strong Christian guidance for you to follow; however, I need to recognize that many have not begun here. Some have come from broken homes, fractured families, abusive situations, or possibly no home life at all. Some may have spent their entire childhood wandering, searching for any form of parental direction. This alone is reason enough to feel as though your compass is completely defective. If this feels familiar to you, firstly, I want to remind you that God is in the business of redemption. He is able to make beauty out of ashes and restore even the most broken of hearts. He can reach you where you are, no matter how far you have been dragged from the safety of the marked trail. It is understandable that someone who has not received proper guidance from family would find themselves disoriented as they approach adulthood.

2. *You veered off the path.* Some of us come from a position of solid direction. Your childhood was relatively secure: you had an education, loving direction, a home, and a strong support system. You have been blessed with an advantageous beginning point to your own journey. Yet even with this solid foundation, you may still find that at some point you have taken a wrong turn. Your state of insecurity is a direct result of a conscious decision to step away from the path your family has led you on for most of your childhood. When we long for independence too soon and become determined to venture on our own against the will of

those who know how to keep us safe, we have to be willing to accept the consequences of losing our bearings.

3. *You lack confidence in your skills.* Throughout our childhood, we walk beside our family, watching how they travel: how they traverse the terrain, overcome the mountains, take in the scenery, and endure the storms. In doing so, we are learning skills necessary for our own journey. The goal in parenting is to pass on these skills to our children in a manner so that they find confidence in their own ability. I am not talking about physical skills, although they are important and much easier to observe, but skills such as prayer, love, compassion, kindness, respect, faith, endurance, and trust. These proficiencies are much more difficult to instill and even more so to ensure their intrinsic value. A lack of confidence in our own skillfulness in these areas is one of the most common ways adults – young and old alike – fail to stand on their own two feet and boldly embark on their path.

4. *You refuse to consult the Trail Guide.* This is probably the most self-destructive reason for not finding our footing. As discussed throughout previous chapters, the only way to be sure that we are where we are supposed to be and we are going where we are intended to go is to stay on the One Path that has been laid out specifically for us by the Father. Without acceptance of this, it will be impossible to ever truly feel as though you are standing on solid ground. Too many times we turn away from God's ways because we want to believe that our way is better. We detour onto our self-made trail, without even a second glance at the Trail Guide provided for us through Jesus Christ. Friend, let me assure you from my own experience with this route that no amount of preparation on our part can promise us a safe passage through life. The only security we can find is in placing our trust in Jesus and being obedient to the guidelines He has set forth for us in His Word.

Once we have realized that we have not started in a true state of lost-ness - but a perception of it - we can begin to work on our next step. Dear Reader, there is no being lost with God. The Father has plotted every inch of your course. Wherever you are is no surprise to Him. If you find that you fall into one of the above categories, please understand that He knows exactly where you are. You may feel as though you have lost your way, yet it is more likely that you have lost your footing. Somewhere as you were beginning your own path to adulthood you became off-balance. Maybe you have become disoriented by your circumstances, you've been pushed down by Satan, or you have stumbled in your Christian walk. Any of these can make us feel unequipped for the journey and afraid to go on.

Not All Who Wander Are Lost

Firstly, we must recognize that the only way to know we are on the course He has set for us is to be a follower of Christ. Accepting that we have been born sinners and that Christ has died for the sake of those sins in order to gain us access to the Father is crucial. When we fail to take this step our risk of getting lost is guaranteed. But when we are redeemed believers we automatically have the surety of His direction. There is surefootedness in our journey when we recognize that we are on the exact path that has been set for us by the Master Navigator.

As I stated before, I have a hard time accepting the phrase *finding oneself*, for I feel that a more accurate depiction for this time in your life is actually *defining yourself*. Once we know who we are in Christ, we have a wonderful opportunity to hone in on who He made us to be, and to explore all that entails. Defining who we are is exhilarating, liberating, and sometimes terrifying.

The question that comes with how we are defining ourselves is who we are allowing to define us. Are you giving permission to anyone other than God to define who you are? When we do this we allow others the ability to place unattainable expectations on us. We begin to try to live up to qualities that were never intended for us and that will only lead to us feeling like a failure.

When I was in high school, the general expectation of my peers was that everyone was going to go to college. I attended a competitive school in an achievement - oriented community. When we graduated no one asked us *if* we were going to go on to college, but *where*. I remember distinctly a classmate who was not as academically inclined as many of his cohorts, yet he was brilliant in mechanics. I don't remember much what he looked like, except that he often had stained jeans and blackened hands. I don't even remember his name. What I can remember was that he walked with his head hung and shoulders slumped. He sat in the back corner of the class, oftentimes drawing aimlessly, working hard to avoid eye contact. I am pretty sure he spent the entirety of his high school years trying to remain unnoticed.

Then one hot June morning he quietly walked across the graduation stage. No excitement. No celebration. I do not recall what he did with his life after high school, but I do recall one important detail of this young man: He became defined by those around him, and when his abilities did not match up with surrounding expectations, he wore his disappointment for all to see. My guess is that not many adults fostered his natural ability to work with his hands. As students, we were constantly reminded that formal education was the only path to success. I am sure that my young friend held every tool necessary to find a successful career, yet he chose to be defined by someone else's expectation. I pray my classmate was able to find his place in the world. I pray that somewhere along the way he realized how talented he was, and that his value was not defined by a college education.

It is so easy and common for us to allow others to define who we are, especially as we enter adulthood. Adolescence leaves us insecure and anxious about who we are and who we will become. It is at this dangerous place when we will believe anyone who has an opinion of who we are. Friends, parents, teachers, employers, church members and even perfect strangers all play a part in forming labels for us. Whether or not it is intentional, it inevitably occurs. Other people's perception of us, combined with our heightened lack of self-awareness, becomes the perfect recipe for confusion and anxiety.

However, there is a way to combat this time of disorientation by putting blinders on to how other people define you and looking only to the One whose definition of you leads you down the correct path for your life. In an article published by Mark Altrogge in *God's Faithfulness*, he explains that

> *The reality is that none of us are secure in the world except in Christ. Nothing is certain....But when we are tempted about the future it is important for us to meditate on these unshakable, always true Bible verses about the future. We can know God is good through the scriptures. In the scriptures, he makes it VERY clear that our future is secure in him.*[8]

We only have to look to one source, and that is our loving Father, who wants nothing more than for us to discover our identity in Him. When we finally recognize and accept that identity, we are able to find sure footing on the path that He has set for us. This is echoed in Psalm 121:3-5: "He will not allow your foot to slip; He who keeps you will not slumber. Behold, He who keeps Israel will neither slumber nor sleep. The LORD is your keeper; The LORD is your shade on your right hand."

What we read, watch, listen to, and believe will all influence our earthly perception of who we are, and when we are not secure in our identity as a Child of God, we easily let those influences mold us. Yet the Bible tells us that we are not that person!

See what great love the Father has lavished on us, that we should be called children of God! And that is what we are! The reason the world does not know us is that it did not know Him. Dear friends, now we are children of God, and what we will be has not yet been made known. But we know that when Christ appears, we shall be like Him, for we shall see Him as He is. (I John 3:1-2 NIV)

Can you believe these words? Do you understand the magnitude of this? Our Father, who created the vast universe, the tallest mountains, and the deepest seas calls us His *child*. Kenneth W. Hagin writes, "When we really understand our identity in Christ - who we are in Him - it changes the way we think and live. Second Corinthians 5:17 (NKJV) says, 'If anyone is in Christ, he is a new creation; old things have passed away; behold, all things have become new.'"[9]

Lifetime success does not come from being who other people want us to be or who we think we ought to be. Instead, assurance comes from realizing our full potential as a child of the King and resting in the knowledge that no matter where life takes us, we can stand firm in our identity through Christ. When we take our first steps onto our individual path, we can step out in confidence, knowing that our footing is secure and our direction is certain.

He who did not spare his own Son but gave him up for us all, how will He not also with him graciously give us all things? (Romans 8:32)

I will instruct you and teach you in the way you should go; I will counsel you with my eye upon you. (Psalm 32:8)

For we walk by faith, not by sight, [living our lives in a manner consistent with our confident belief in God's promises.] (2 Corinthians 5:7)

Travel Notes:

Do you feel lost? If so, what are some areas in life that have you feeling disoriented?

Based on the discussed list, what reason is causing you to feel lost?

Who or what are you allowing to define you? Are these positive or negative influences?

How can you find confidence in your role as a Child of God? What assurance does He promise to you?

7

Soil Analysis - Environment

Therefore, as you received Christ Jesus the Lord, so walk in Him, rooted and built up in Him and established in the faith, just as you were taught; abounding in thanksgiving. Colossians 2:6-7[10]

For the past decade or two, I have had the privilege of witnessing my friends' children, as well as my own, go from mischievous toddlers to unique, confident, incredible adults. Although the end result has been primarily successful, the process has been somewhat strenuous. The common theme is that childhood is HARD. We are placed in situations which, although God-ordained, may not seem like the right place for us. We each have gone through times in our lives when we just did not feel as though we fit into our family, school, church, friends, the list can go on. Yet as a child, our options for change are limited. We cannot typically change families, schools, or churches. These are decisions that are out of a child's hands.

Due to this, we often struggle as youth to adapt, and in turn we learn important life lessons on how to get along with others and do our best in any circumstance. However, let us not diminish how difficult this task is. Childhood is filled with trudging through situations that make us uncomfortable and often feel as though we have been planted in the wrong soil.

There is a popular saying "Bloom where you are planted." We see this phrase on social media and hanging in classrooms and churches. Although I believe in this concept and encourage young people to make the best of where God has placed them, I also believe that sometimes we are simply in soil that is difficult for our growth. I recently ran across a phrase by Alexander Den Heijer that caught my eye - "When a flower doesn't bloom, you fix the environment in which it grows, not the flower."

As the mother of a teenage daughter, this spoke volumes to me, and frankly, humbled me. For quite some time, I had been searching and praying for what to teach my daughter in order to make her a better woman. I had been trying to change her behavior in an effort to help her thrive, despite her teenage struggles. What God showed me through this simple sentence was that I needed to figure out what soil she would thrive in, not force her to grow in poor soil.

As parents, I will admit that we are limited in our abilities at times. Actually, most of the time. We read books, consult experts, seek out those who have gone before, and take it to God in prayer, yet we find ourselves flawed and inadequate at best. See, we are not perfect parents. There is only One perfect Parent, and as an earthly parent our only true job is to point our children to Him. However, even knowing this, we still attempt to parent our children into being "good kids." We use what we learned from our own parents and our own lives to try to mold our children into what we believe to be the best for them.

It is here in this place that I found myself losing sleep and wringing my hands to figure out how to parent my daughter into being the best woman she could be. I was looking to check off the list of desirable character traits for a young woman, to see her succeed in the way I envisioned for her. And there it was: in the way *I* envisioned. Ouch. As I saw her grapple with life's ups and downs, I longed for her to "bloom where she was planted." I thought I had the answers to achieve this. Struggling with friends? Find ways to get along. Trouble with school? Dig deep and work harder. Disappointing circumstances? Cry it out and move on. Then I was reminded - "When a flower doesn't bloom, you fix the environment in which it grows, not the flower." My daughter didn't need to handle life like I do because she is not me. I was trying to fix the flower.

The Right Spot

When my mother-in-law passed away, we were gifted a hydrangea plant at her funeral. We planted it in the flower bed near to my front door. It is a spot that I pass to enter my home, so I thought it would be a nice reminder of her each day. This location receives many hours of sun, especially in the afternoon. For several years we watched this bush struggle to survive. The leaves were spindly, it failed to fill out, and it rarely produced good blooms, if any at all. My husband finally came to me one summer and suggested that we move the bush to another location on our property. After researching its needs, we discovered that it needed plentiful shade and thrived in morning sunlight. Oops. We immediately relocated it to the other side of our home where it would have a much higher chance of surviving and thriving.

Our lives are similar to my hydrangea bush. Sometimes, we start out in a harsh environment. My poor hydrangea was just barely hanging on all these years. It was thirsty, scorched, and struggling to survive, let alone bloom. Our lives can easily begin this way. We may not be in an environment that is easy for us to thrive. Sometimes our failure to thrive doesn't quite make sense; our families and friends try their best to care for us and nurture us, just like I did my plant. Yet even so, sometimes our situations leave us feeling like we are struggling to hang on, and we often cringe when people mention that we should be blooming.

Although it is important to mention that we should always be pushing ourselves to be our very best in any situation, it is also important to note that some environments are simply not conducive to our optimum growth. Was my hydrangea still alive? Yes. Was it producing blooms? Most of the time. Yet I would definitely not say that my plant was flourishing by any means, or even coming close to its beautiful potential.

Friends, oftentimes, especially through our teenage years, we feel as though we are not good enough. We look at our lives and wonder why we can't get it all together and where we have gone wrong. We internalize our differences and place blame on ourselves when we struggle with one area of our lives or another. One of the first things we can do to combat these feelings of inadequacy is to look around us.

Assess our environment. By doing this, we can begin to diagnose why we are not growing to our full potential. Let's look at some questions we can ask ourselves:

1. *Where am I planted?* Is my current environment best for healthy growth? Am I content with where I live, who I live with, etc.? If your answer to this is "No, I am not in a good home environment," then you may need to assess your options. Are you still living at home and dependent on your parents, guardian, or spouse for your livelihood? If this is the case, you may be unable to change your current situation. If you are not dependent on a family member, then maybe ask yourself if there are changes that you need to make in your living conditions. If where you are living or who you are living with is not a nurturing environment for you, then a change of address may be in order.

2. *What am I surrounded with?* Take a look around. Who are the people you share life with? Who do you encounter daily that influences your life? It may be friends, family members, or co-workers. Are the people who are surrounding you aiding in your growth, or hindering it? Again, we have to ask ourselves if change can be made. If a physical separation is necessary and possible, this may be the time to make a change.

Throughout life there will be times when those around us leave us parched for water or burnt up in the sun. Sometimes they may even strangle us with their toxic weeds. I have seen friends blame themselves for troubles that have been a result of unhealthy relationships. It is essential that we assess our relationships often and decide if they are helping us to produce our finest blooms. And when they are not, we have to make tough choices on whether it is time for us to seek a different soil.

We cannot always alter our physical relationships with family and co-workers; however, we can alter our emotional ones. You are in control of your own mind and emotions. If someone is unhealthy, you must make a strong resolve to not allow them to influence you any longer. This will often times take great strength and maturity, both of which can be found in Jesus Christ. Praying to Him and asking Him to protect your mind from negative influences and to properly guide you in your relationships is a huge step to gaining independence and growth.

3. *Am I getting the proper elements?* We all know that for plants to survive, they must have three essential elements: light, air, and water. We possess very similar needs, of course scientifically, but more importantly, spiritually. In order for us to maintain proper growth and produce beautiful blooms, we must feed our hearts with the proper elements. We begin to see evidence of our dependence on a divine source of life from the very beginning: "Then the LORD God formed a man from the dust of the ground and breathed into his nostrils the breath of life, and the man became a living thing" (Genesis 2:7 NIV). It was God Himself who breathed life into the first man and who continues to breathe life into us today.

We see these analogies throughout the entirety of both the Old and New Testament. A Psalmist declares to the Father, "They [Your children] are abundantly satisfied with the fullness of Your house, And You give them drink from the river of Your pleasures. For with You is the fountain of life; In Your light we see light" (Psalm 36:8-9). Jesus often referred to these essential elements when He spoke of Himself in the New Testament, "I am the light of the world. Whoever follows me will never walk in darkness, but will have the light of life" (John 8:12 NIV).

Jesus knew that we can relate to our need for these life-giving items. In one such occasion, Jesus visited a Samaritan woman at a well and spoke directly to her need of life-giving sustenance.

> *When a Samaritan woman came to draw water, Jesus said to her, "Will you give me a drink?" (His disciples had gone into the town to buy food.) The Samaritan woman said to him, "You are a Jew and I am a Samaritan woman. How can you ask me for a drink?" (For Jews do not associate with Samaritans.) Jesus answered her, "If you knew the gift of God and who it is that asks you for a drink, you would have asked him and he would have given you living water." "Sir," the woman said, "you have nothing to draw with and the well is deep. Where can you get this living water? Are you greater than our father Jacob, who gave us the well and drank from it himself, as did also his sons and his livestock?" Jesus answered, "Everyone who drinks this water will be thirsty again, but whoever drinks the water I give them will never thirst. Indeed, the water I give them will become in them a spring of water welling up to eternal life." (John 4:7-14)*

Obviously, God knew that equating Himself with the physical items that we depend on for survival would speak loudly to us, as there are many more references found throughout the Bible. We cannot allow their significance to be lost on us. The message clearly states that God is the life-line to our very being, and we are completely dependent upon Him. Without Him as our air, light, and water, we will quickly become spiritually malnourished. Even when we believe that we have chosen the right environment for our success in life, we need to access the life-giving elements provided to feed our hearts and souls. The most beautiful and hearty plant will still wither if not given access to oxygen, light, and water. It matters not how strong we are; we cannot survive without tapping into Him for spiritual vitality.

The Great Provider

Our environment may not be entirely up to us. We may find ourselves in situations that seem hopeless for us to thrive in. I want to encourage you today that no place is beyond the reach of our Father's hand. He sees you and cares about where you are. He knows everything about your struggles and your challenges. There is no place on this earth hidden from Him. King David marvels at God's ability in this in Psalm 139.

> Is there any place I can go to avoid your Spirit? To be out of your sight? If I climb to the sky, you're there! If I flew on the morning's wings to the far western horizon, You'd find me in a minute – you're already there waiting! Then I said to myself, "Oh, he even sees me in the dark! At night I'm immersed in the light!" It's a fact: darkness isn't dark to you; night and day, darkness and light, they're all the same to you. (Psalm 139:7-12 The Message)

With this knowledge, He also possesses the ability to give you what you need to thrive, and He is generous in providing that for you. I know it is difficult to have confidence in what we cannot see. It is easy for us to talk the talk when it comes to trusting that God will provide for us, but when we are faced with real life hardship - the kind that is so thick with desperation that we cannot seem to find our way out of it – is when we are called to walk the walk of faith. That is the true essence of faith. Believing in what we cannot see; believing that, although we may not be living in an ideal environment for us, God is still in control and has the ability to help us to thrive.

One of the passages of Scripture that has sustained me throughout my life is in the Gospel of Matthew. It has always struck me as so simple, yet so profound. When I first encountered these verses, it was a "duh" moment for me, as if I should have figured this out. Yet, this is the beauty in Scripture: It points us to the simplicity of God's provision for us. We tend to complicate things - well, at least I do. We think that what we need is too hard for even Him. We feel that the despair of our situation is too much for anyone to surmount. We hesitate to believe that there is a way out of the dark of our circumstance and into the light of His provision. Let's take a look at these verses and see if we can gain a bit of insight into the simplicity of why we can trust in Him:

> *Therefore I tell you, do not be anxious about your life, what you will eat or what you will drink, nor about your body, what you will put on. Is not life more than food, and the body more than clothing? Look at the birds of the air: they neither sow nor reap nor gather into barns, and yet your heavenly Father feeds them. Are you not of more value than they? And which of you by being anxious can add a single hour to his span of life? And why are you anxious about clothing? Consider the lilies of the field, how they grow: they neither toil nor spin, yet I tell you, even Solomon in all his glory was not arrayed like one of these. (Matthew 6:25-34 NIV)*

Do you see? Look around at the wonder of creation and realize that there is only One being who has put this all into motion. Do you think the trees worry when they drop their leaves whether or not they will return? Or if the squirrels worry about where they will find their nuts and seeds to sustain them through the winter? Nature is a wonderful reminder that God provides for all of His creation – and are you not that much more precious to Him? In my days of worry and despair I cling to these verses to speak into me of His love and care for me. He will not allow me to fail, as long as I lean into Him and trust in His ways.

Your environment may not be where you had envisioned yourself. Your dreams may currently be dwindled to literal nightmares. You may have abandoned all hope of rising out of the toxic soil that is poisoning you. Yet let me remind you that He is in the business of seeing our need, knowing our desires, and raising us up out of despair into the warm, nourishing soil of His glory. He longs to see us blossom into the radiant fullness that lies in Him. Although you may not be able to physically change your environment, God has the ability to bring life-giving change for you to thrive.

Our Resting Place

Remember at the beginning of the chapter when I mentioned my friends' children? There is one child in particular that I have had the privilege of watching blossom into a unique, beautiful young adult. Throughout this young lady's life, she has always marched to the beat of her own drum. Amazingly passionate, naturally sensitive, and generously giving of herself and all she has. She has inarguably been an individual who has challenged life and those around her with fervor. Having such a charismatic personality has not always been the easiest for her throughout her youth, and she has most definitely faced emotional and spiritual challenges. Yet, through all of that, there was one phrase that always jumped out to me: she needs to find her people.

When we go through childhood, we are surrounded by peers, not by choice, but by circumstance. We do not get to choose who we share a Sunday school class or homeroom with. It would be naïve of us to believe that everyone we are surrounded by in our school years creates the ideal environment for our growth. I tell you this to encourage you if you are in this place where you are feeling as though no one around you understands you; if you are lonely and isolated, please remember that there does come a time in our lives when we will find our "people."

At some point in our lives, we finally have the opportunity to seek out those who we feel help us to grow and thrive. They are the ones who fuel us with passion for our career, ministry, hobbies, or life in general. They might be friends, co-workers, a church family, or a spouse. When we find the right environment, we feel as though we have discovered our resting place. Who we are and what we desire begins to make sense. The pieces that at one time seemed awkward and misshapen finally fall into place to create a beautiful image.

So what became of my young friend? Well, although she is still working to find her place in this world, she has begun to find her people. She discovered an area of work that she is passionate about and, as often happens, she has became more confident in herself. She works hard because she loves what she is doing. She found an environment that suited her personality and nurtured her spirit. It has been beautiful to watch her begin to grow and bloom into a strong young woman.

There is no perfect environment for us to thrive in. No matter where we are planted, we must work hard to become who God desires of us to be. There will always be weeds, toxic influences, and harsh elements to contend with. Yet, when we place our trust in Christ to provide for us, and know that in time He will direct us towards those who feed us emotionally and spiritually, we can have hope that one day soon we will find our resting place. Just like my hydrangea, we will find our sweet spot, the one place that gives us the ideal conditions for us to not only grow, but also to thrive and burst into the bountiful beauty that our Creator intended for us.

Travel Notes:

As it pertains to your current environment, ask yourself the following 3 questions:

1. Where am I planted?
2. What am I surrounded with?
3. Am I getting the proper elements?

Is there anything in your environment that needs to change? Are you fighting weeds or toxic influences? If so, what is it and are you in a position to make a change?

Who can you seek out to help you grow and thrive? Pray to God to make those influences clear to you.

What areas in your life can you see God's provision? Praise Him for those areas!

8

Separation Anxiety - For Parents

But Jesus said, "Let the little children come to me, and do not hinder them, for to such belongs the kingdom of heaven." Matthew 19:14[11]

Preparing to loosen our tie to our children can be a scary and emotional time for a parent. We must first possess trust to set them on their own path, trust that our parenting has done its job, and trust that they are ready to be on their own. My feeling is that typically the latter comes before the former. Most young adults come equipped with an internal gauge that signals them for the beginning of their adult journey, and it also instills the confidence in them that they need in order to make the move away from their parents. It is our job as their parents to encourage them during this time by reinforcing their independence and demonstrating our confidence in them (even if it isn't always there).

Although our young adults seem ready to venture out on their own path, there is hesitation and anxiety there as well. Most do not wish for their parent to see this apprehension, and so will seek reassurance and advice from outside sources. Here is where it is important to encourage your child to find a Godly mentor or guide to help them navigate these early years of adulthood (See Chapter 9: Sherpas). It is vital that you recognize that your child may not come to you for assistance during these first years of adulthood, and to resolve to not allow it to cause hurt and separation between you. Let us look at several reasons a child may desire separation from their parent as a young adult:

1) *They want to appear capable in the eyes of the parent.* They long to prove that they are, in fact, ready for this monumental phase in their lives, and thus will avoid sharing their fears and failures with their parent as they branch out. This desire for approval and drive to succeed can be overwhelmingly strong in many young adults. As a parent, it is of utmost importance that we do not encourage their fear by appearing condescending to the young adult. It is understood that our children are going to make mistakes, especially during this time.

Remember when your child was learning to walk? Those little chubby legs would waddle around the house, a look of sheer determination on his/her face, only to wobble and plop over every few steps. That toddler was unbalanced and uncertain, but resolute to make it to the destination. Young adults are no different. As they head out on their path, the way is unclear, they are unbalanced from the weight of their backpack full of God's resources for them to use along the way, and uncertain as to exactly how they are supposed to get there. But their determination to reach a destination is present still the same. Just as you were the biggest cheerleader for that small child, you need to again be the biggest cheerleader for your young adult. They need to know that someone is in their corner, believing in them and supporting them. What they do not need is someone to call them out when they falter, or shake their head in disappointment when they fall. Young adults will fail. That is where the learning occurs. Our job as parents is to know when to step in to help set them on their feet again, and when to let them pull themselves up and keep waddling along.

To the parent who always picks their children up, I want to offer a little word of caution. When children learn to walk, parents must be careful to not rush to their side with every wobble and spill. As tempting as it was to want to pick them up, dust them off, and set them on their way again, we learned early on that they needed to do this for themselves. They needed to fall in order to learn how to find the proper balance to stand and walk alone. This same principle applies to young adults. If parents constantly rush to pick up children who falter, these young adults may never learn how to find success alone. Here is where we find adults who may always be searching for a path where someone else will lead them. This is dangerous ground that we will address in a later chapter. My only encouragement would be to allow your children to fail. Although it is hard to watch at times, it is important for their growth. Just as Christ allows us to wobble and spill in order to point us to Him, in the same way, young adults often find Him in the mud puddles of life. God uses our failures in order for us to see our desperate need for Him. We must be cautious not to stand in the way of God's same work in them.

2.) *They fail to recognize the value in their parent.* As much as this one pains us as parents, it is very real for many families. I have seen over and over young adults who still believe that their parent could not possibly understand or possess knowledge about what they are going through. And frankly, I can remember a day when I was a naïve teen who held the same misbeliefs. This is part of the growth process. A wise parent will recognize this as a way for their child to learn how to stand on their own two feet, instead of becoming offended or hurt. We all dream of the day when our children realize our value and long to soak up our wisdom, but frankly, that day is sometimes long-coming, or may never arrive. We pray that the years and tears that have been poured into their upbringing result in adults who appreciate the efforts put forth to make them a valuable contribution to society and who we can be proud of. Know, Dear Parent, that God recognizes and blesses those efforts, even when our children do not.

Once we can accept that our children are beginning a process of separation with us, and recognize its importance in allowing them to successfully transition into adulthood, we need to then assess our role and responsibility. Our goal as parents is to work ourself out of a job. The more we understand what this entails, the better equipped we are to assist our child as we work towards this goal. Letting our children venture into adulthood is traumatic. Let us look at why this transition is so difficult and ask God to open our eyes to how we can work to ease some of the discomfort.

The Tether

When I used to take my small children hiking, they were too little to walk so they would ride on my back in a carrier. I would strap on the baby backpack, hoist my child into the seat, and sling the pack onto my back. It was a feat in and of itself to just get the pack on and strapped without dumping my sweet, wiggling child upside down. We would head out on the trail, their little legs dangling out of the holes, kicking me in the back, their hands smacking me in the head – often to the rhythm of some silly song – and me, sweating, unbalanced, and tripping over rocks and roots from the burden of the extra weight. It was quite a task, but one that I willingly conquered to keep them safe on the trail. Early parenting is just the same. We keep those little ones close to us and under tight protection, no matter the cost. It is necessary for their safety and well-being.

As my children became a little older and more sure-footed, I advanced to having the child wear a backpack with a long strap. When we hiked, my small child could have the freedom of walking the trail, but was always within my grasp. This tether system kept them within my reach as they learned their boundaries. Figuratively, this is where our children stay for the majority of their childhood. We keep them on a loose rope, always safely within our reach but able to find their boundaries in life. We allow them to experience successes and failures, yet we maintain the ability to rescue them if they fall. We keep them close to us so that we can keep them on our path. They are part of our family unit, so we travel together and they follow where we lead.

At the time of this writing, there was a young boys' soccer team in Thailand that chose to go exploring one afternoon after practice. The coach and players walked several miles into a cave. Soon it began to rain, and due to monsoon season, the cave they were in quickly filled with water, preventing their exit. After ten days the boys were finally discovered by Navy seals, but they were unable to be rescued by the divers. The only way to get the boys out was a nine-hour journey that required them to Scuba dive for hours at a time. None of the boys could swim. In the end, the Navy seals spent days teaching the boys to dive, and eventually escorted three boys at a time out of the cave. Each boy was tethered to two divers – one in front who carried their oxygen tank, and one behind them to help them along and keep them safe. They were all attached to a rope system that stretched across the entire path to the exit. Miraculously, all thirteen young men were rescued over the course of several days.

This is our job as parents. We tie our children to us – one parent in front (the leader and supplier) and one in back (the one who ensures safety). We carry their supplies willingly, to lift the burden off of them so that they can focus on getting to the destination safely. Interestingly, the divers had to swim without flippers, leaving them at a major disadvantage for the journey, but necessary to avoid injuring the young boys. In the same way we often have to sacrifice our own comfort for the sake of our children, even when it makes our journey much more difficult.

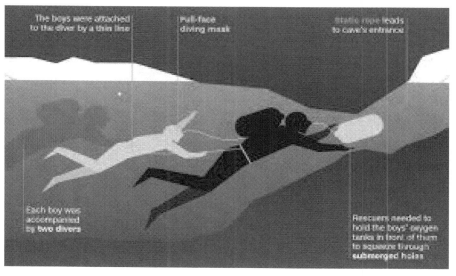

The boys were attached to the diver by a thin line

Full-face diving mask

static rope leads to cave's entrance

Each boy was accompanied by two divers

Rescuers needed to hold the boys' oxygen tanks in front of them to squeeze through submerged holes

12

One other element that was essential for the rescue of the boys was a guide rope that traveled the length of the entire journey. The divers and rescuees attached themselves to this rope, so that even in the muddiest, deepest waters, they were able to find their way out. God is just such a guide rope for us. Hopefully, we have tethered ourselves to Him. He is our lifeline, the only One who knows the path. He provides us a rope to cling to, even when we cannot clearly see the way. As a family, we need to be fastened to His rope, and we need to make sure that our children are as well. "These commandments that I give you today are to be on your hearts. Impress them on your children. Talk about them when you sit at home and when you walk along the road, when you lie down and when you get up" (Deuteronomy 6:6-7 NIV).

To single parents: I understand that parenting alone brings on a multitude of challenges. If you have been raising your child alone, I realize that you may feel overwhelmed by the above image, thinking that you have had to carry the load of two rescuers: You have had to carry the life-giving equipment and also ensure the safety of your child. May I bring to you the assurance that you have not been alone. Jesus has been beside you, filling in the gaps for you. Christ longs to come along beside you and aid you in your parenting. Whenever you feel weak, He is there to share your load. I pray you are able to surrender some of that load to Him, with full confidence in His ability to ensure your child is not left behind, and that you have the strength you need to carry him/her into adulthood.

So often we believe that we can pull our children through life. We do our best to navigate our family's path, and we feel confident in our ability to safely survive the journey. If we attempt to parent our children without the assistance of God, we take a significant risk with our family. Parenting without the presence of God is like those divers swimming through the system of caves without a guide rope. They could easily become disoriented and lose their way. The water was murky and not easy for them to see the direction they needed to go, despite the level of skill they possessed. If there is ever a time in our lives when we experience murky waters, raising children is that time! All of the parenting books and knowledge are useless if we cannot see where we are going. It is essential that we firmly harness ourselves to Him, so that in any circumstance and unfamiliar terrain, we are never far from His path for us. We can find assurance in our direction as parents when we know the One who has laid the path for us.

Loosening the Rope

Although we spend the best part of our children's lives with that loving tether connecting us, there comes a time when we no longer need to tether our children to us. This is when parenting gets scary for so many. Typically this time comes when our children reach the ages of teens to early twenties. As aforementioned, youth possess an internal ability to feel when this time is coming. Hopefully, parents are in tune with their child enough to also feel their readiness. That may not always be the case. It is then when a parent has to trust in their parenting and in their child. Not an easy thing to do.

Young adults need to find their own path. Around this time they need to leave the path of their parents, strap on their pack, and begin their own journey. Prayerfully, they are believers and have a desire to seek the Lord's destination for their lives. If your child is not a believer, then this needs to be your first step as they leave your path. As you watch your unbelieving child begin their life, your prayers for their salvation are the strongest support you can offer to them. Along with this, I firmly believe in the power of a parent's petition for God to protect them in their unbelief. Although I was saved at a very young age, I have heard many stories of adults whose testimony involves God protecting them from their sinful decisions, even though they did not believe in Him. Our God is a merciful God, and wants nothing more than to please His people. Our children's decisions may not lead them where He wants them to go, and it may be a very painful process to watch; however, I feel strongly that our God hears the hearts of praying parents and can bless us with peace.

Parenting Styles

As we navigate through this tumultuous and often unpredictable time, we often find that we, as parents, gravitate to one style of parenting or another. I want to be forthright in stating that there is no condemnation for parents of young adults. Everyone enters this stage differently, and I am convinced that if you are reading this page, you have nothing but good intentions, concern, and love for your child. With that said, there are different ways that we can approach parenting this age group, so let us look at the characteristics of those styles.

Clean Cut

This parent is ready to cut their child loose. They have full confidence in his/her ability to enter adult life and trust in the steadfastness of God to lead their young person. This parent helps their child to see the value in the gifts and talents that God has provided them, helps them strap on their backpack full of those resources, and sends them on their way down the path. This parent is an encourager and supporter of their child. They see the uncertainties that lie ahead and, instead of fearing for their child's safety, realize that he/she is fastened to the ultimate Guide Rope. They also understand that when their child encounters rough terrain, they will be there, not to pull them through it or rescue them from it, but to offer them their God-given resources to help him/her conquer that part of the journey. This is a parenting goal, to be sure. The desire of our hearts as parents should be to see our children successfully take to their own path, full of confidence and solidly rooted to God.

Survival of the Fittest

This is the "sink or swim" parent. My husband's grandfather used to throw his young grandsons into the swimming pool in full expectation that they would learn to swim out of sheer necessity for survival. This parent often maintains this philosophy into their child's journey into adulthood. They disconnect quickly from their child and operate under the premise of survival of the fittest. Although it is healthy to trust in your parenting and in the capabilities of your child, it can be dangerous when we assume that our children can conquer their journey without our assistance. I have seen often in my work with young adults the parents who refuse to give any form of "hand-out" to their child, because they were most likely not given any as they became adults. The intention is to make their child strong by them having to independently survive, yet this may lead to the young adult feeling abandoned. This feeling of abandonment could possibly result in the young adult feeling incompetent and fearful of failing. It is crucial that we assess each child and their response to this process. If we recognize that our young adult is overcome with anxiety, hesitates to make life decisions, or lacks self-confidence, we need to evaluate how we can increase our level of guidance in order to build up their confidence and self-reliance.

Attachment Disorders

It is extremely easy as parents to wrap our entire existence around our children. We have dedicated the past 18+ years of life to raising and guiding them. In fact, we can't even remember what it feels like to walk our path without them. I remember when my children were old enough to stay home alone. I reveled in my ability to run to the grocery store by myself. As a homeschooler of four, my time spent without at least one or more children was a very rare occurrence. So naturally, I took advantage of this freedom at any chance I could get. What I soon found out, however, was that I spent the entire time in the store looking for my kids. It was such an oddity for me to not be looking underfoot and down the aisles to make sure they were safe and accounted for.

In the same way, when our children grow up and begin to leave our homes, it is common to have a period of adjustment to not being "on guard" at all times. As a parent, we are never off duty to our children. We want to know that they are safe and accounted for. The more independent they become, we find ourselves out of a job, and for many parents, that can be a nerve-wracking and emotional experience. However, there is risk for the parent who fails to allow their young adult to find their own path. Some parents have tread so deeply into the parenting role, that they have lost sight of their own path. Somewhere along the way, the child became the leader of their parent's journey and when that child leaves the home, the parent finds himself/herself completely lost.

It is vital for us as parents to have sure footing in our own path as we begin adulthood and eventually parenthood. We must have confidence that our path is ordained by God solely for us, so that if anyone leaves our path, we will not be dismayed or lost. Too many adults have failed to recognize and follow God's path for their individual lives, and when they become parents, they allow their path to be merged with their child(ren)'s. The danger here is when the young adult is ready to branch off, the parent desires to come along. They have strayed from their own path so far that they seek security in their child's path. We see this in parents who insist on being a central part of their young adult's life. This could possibly lead to the young adult feeling smothered and unable to begin his life for fear of hurting his parent's feelings. This also thwarts the progress in the child's path because he is having to accommodate for having the parent along for the journey.

As I have stated, I am a homeschooling mother. My time and energy that is devoted to my children on a daily basis is exhausting yet very fulfilling. I could easily say that my children are my life. But I have to choose not to. I want to be very careful to put my Father God and His path for *my* life first. I have to remember that I was a child of God before I was a mother. God began my path when I became an adult and He has a specific destination for me, Shawna, not for me, mother of four. My identity must be in my own journey and where He wants me to go and how He wants me to get there.

I cannot confuse my path with that of my children. As much as I love being part of their lives and sharing my every day with them, their time with me is limited and I must recognize them as independent travelers. They have to discover God's destination for their journey, and although I can walk alongside of them in rough terrain or celebrate the scenic views with them, their journey is not mine and I cannot come along.

Failure to Disconnect

Watching our kids walk away from us and onto their own path is harrowing at best. It is scary and worrisome. It is potentially one of the most difficult moments in parenting. This fear often drives a parent into an inability to let go of their young adult. Often we see a parent who does not want disconnect the tether. They long to hold on in an attempt to protect their child. They feel that their young adult needs their constant involvement and guidance. This stems from an ultimate mistrust in God as their child's guide. In I Timothy 1:9 God tells us that fear is of not of Him: "For God hath not given us the spirit of fear; but of power, and of love, and of a sound mind" (KJV).

In the same way that God has equipped us for our journey, He has equipped our children. A denial of His provision for either ourselves or our children is against Him and is sinful. Doubting our children's ability is in reality denying God's ability to lead our children.

When we refuse to disconnect emotionally from our young adult, the consequence can be painful for both the parent and child. Imagine a rope tether from a parent to a child. When that child begins to take their own path, tension occurs in the rope. As the parent attempts to stay on their path and the young adult branches off, there are two scenarios that can occur.

1. *The young adult becomes hindered.* The tether that is put into place in parenting is only so long. When that rope tightens and the parent insists on staying on their own path, the young person is prevented from moving forward. When a parent fails to disconnect emotionally from the child, yet sends the child down her own path, progress in the young adult's life is hindered. Think of it as tying yourself to a tree and then attempting to run as far as you can. You will only go so far before the rope tightens and you are jerked backwards. In the same way, when parents refuse to untie themselves from their young adult, the young adult becomes hindered by the parent and is unable to explore what God has designed for her life. This hindrance can cause the child to become angry at the parent for standing in the way of her living her life to the fullest. It is important that parents recognize God's ability to lead young adults, and to not stand in the way of that.

2. *The young adult drags the parent through the woods.* When the parent is insistent on remaining attached to a young adult who is determined to begin their own journey in life, the young person will forge down their path regardless of the parent. This strong determination will often result in the young adult continuing on in life while the parent is dragged along by the tightened tether. As one would expect, a parent who hangs on unnecessarily may find himself or herself clinging on for dear life as the child plows through life. The child may potentially lash out in anger or resentment toward the parent. This may result in a parent feeling as though their efforts to help their child go unnoticed or unappreciated, thus further leaving the parent feeling battered and

bruised by their child. A forced connection between the parent and child tends to be unhealthy, dangerous, and hurtful for both parties.

Any person who has walked the road of parenting knows that it is not a journey for the faint of heart. It is unpredictable. One moment we are running through sweet fields of beautiful flowers, and the next we are swinging on one of those long, wobbly suspension bridges, seemingly miles above secure ground. It can seem as though all it takes is one step onto an unstable rung and all of our efforts plunge to the river below. There is no safe path, no guarantee, in parenting. The reason for this is that we are not perfect parents. There is only One who is perfect, and every effort we expend pales in comparison to Him. Yet, I praise Him that He allows us to see this discord, for it is in our recognition of our failures that we see how much we need the hand of an infallible Father, to lead both us and our children. I believe that it is His design to give our children flawed parents so that they will be pointed to their need for Him. It is our job as their parents to admit to our inadequacy and turn their dependence on Him.

When They Disappear

When my son was about twelve, we went hiking with some friends, as often was the case. About ¾ of a mile from the parking lot, the three older boys spotted an appealing embankment that just cried out to be explored. Being preteen boys, they saw the challenge and quickly accepted it. The rugged path looked so much more exciting than the safe path those of us with the small children were taking. Knowing that all three boys were skilled in hiking and possessed good common sense, I encouraged them to take off on their own path and eventually meet up with us at the parking lot. For a while, we could hear them traipsing through the woods – twigs snapping, leaves rustling, boys laughing. But then we not only lost sight of them, we could no longer hear them.

It was a fairly straight shot to the parking area of this small state park, so I knew that they were headed in the correct general direction. Or I hoped they were. My friend became a bit anxious, but we continued on our path. Although I was anticipating their success, I also had faith that God had His eye on them when I did not. As we approached the end of the trail, the boys suddenly dropped onto the path from the woods above. They were a bit messy and had a few scratches and bruises, but they were still laughing and obviously proud of themselves

Some parents lose sight of their kids around their late teens/early twenties. Their children head out on their own path – seemingly the harder one – and they watch them disappear into the unknown wood. I can only imagine that it is nothing short of a terrifying time for a parent. Anxiety sets in. However, we need to rest in the knowledge that God has His eye on them, even when we cannot. We need to hope that they rely on their God-given skills and that they are headed in the correct general direction.

But life isn't like a hike through a small state park. It isn't always a straight path, and there are many hidden dangers. We will not always anticipate their success. And they may disappear for a very long time. Yet we can still have faith that God's eyes are on them. Jesus knows your child by name and is watching over him or her unceasingly. "See, I have engraved you on the palms of my hands; your walls are ever before me" (Isaiah 49:16 NIV). Not one of His children are beyond His reach. We can still trust that He can bring them safely back onto the right path. They may be messy, full of scratches and bruises, but hopefully they can come out stronger and full of pride in their accomplishment.

When I was a young mother, I witnessed a dear friend watch her children walk away from God's path. With fervor they turned their backs on their parents and on God and resolved to take their own path through the woods. It was a time of pain and heartache for this dear mother. Yet, in the darkness, God whispered a sweet truth to me: "If I, God, am the perfect parent and I have wayward children all over the earth, why would I expect any flawed human to be a perfect parent?" Whoa! This was a mighty revelation to me.

Although this does not give us liberty to throw up a white flag under the precipice of naturally flawed parenting, this does allow us to give ourselves a little grace. God knows who we are and what we are capable of as parents. He does not make mistakes in placing our children into our family. He has full faith in us as their parents, and will equip us with everything we need to guide and protect them. Where we are lacking, He fills in the gaps for us. He will not allow your child to get lost without every resource necessary for their return. Trust in His provision and your peace.

Parent, God has your child, but your job is not done. There is nothing more powerful than a praying parent. I know many a mother or father with war-torn knees from hours spent before the Throne. Please never cease praying for your child, no matter what the age or stage in his or her life. Rob Flood in *Children Need Praying Parents* encourages:

> *Pursue your children with great fervor. Pursue God on your children's behalf all the more. This is the type of sacrificial love and prayer our children need to see, feel, and experience from all of us. If our children succeed in life, let us thank God for His great work in their lives. If they wander into the things of this world, let it not be because their mom and dad failed to plead with God on their behalf. And, if and when they return, let us again turn our thanks and praise to God Himself, who is the great Father of us all.*[13]

And Young Person, if you have decided to take the hard trail and you have lost sight of those who love you, remember that God has His eyes on you. He knows exactly where you are and where you need to go. He sees the trees and mud and thorns and is willing to navigate you through it. You may get messy and scratched and bruised, but in the end, He will drop you right where you need to be, and you will be beaming with pride in your success. However, you have to rely on Him! If you have chosen that path – the one less traveled, the one more dangerous – then you must accept what may be lying in wait up on that embankment. Sometimes our flesh sees something appealing and cries out to accept the challenge. There is an inherent risk involved, so hiker beware! However, if you do find yourself in a thorny situation, God will always be there to show you the way back to Him. Remember the words of God in Deuteronomy 31:6, "Be strong and courageous. Do not be afraid or terrified because of them, for the Lord your God goes with you; He will never leave you nor forsake you."

III

Divine Intersections

9

Diving into the Current - Community of Believers

And let us consider how we can spur one another on towards love and good deeds, not giving up meeting together, as some are in the habit of doing, but encouraging one another - and all the more as you see the Day approaching. Hebrews 10:24-25[14]

One beautiful summer day, I took my children to one of our favorite river spots. Hidden from passers-by, it was an area of the river where there were many slick rocks, which made for a perfect sliding rock experience. Many locals braved the rugged river to slip into the current and ride the smooth, slippery rocks all the way to the bottom of the waterfall. Most days, the river was mild and began as almost a trickle at the top of the waterfall, only to end in a shallow pool at the bottom. This particular day, however, the river was high from recent rains, and was flowing much deeper and faster than we had experienced before. This was a fun twist on our old stomping ground, and we were excited to ride down the river faster than ever!

Typically when we have visited the sliding rock, my children knew the safe places to enter and exit the flow of water, which path to avoid as they were sliding down the rock, and how to duck in just the right way to avoid gashing their head on one overhanging rock. It sounds dangerous, doesn't it? It definitely was not for the faint of heart, yet I used it often as a training ground for my kids. They knew the inherent risks that came with this activity. We discussed being alert, being careful, and being willing to assume the risk. I love an opportunity to let nature teach my children much better than I ever could.

On this day, the river widened higher than normal, and the waterfall was plentiful at the very top of the rocks. This was unfamiliar territory for us, as we weren't sure how the current would take us if we entered the river this high up. We quickly discovered that the current pushed us to the other side of the flow of water near the rock wall. My eldest son, Sam (6'3" at the time), attempted this path first and found himself caught in a strong current that led to an undesired location. Luckily, he was big enough to wade back across the current to our side of the river.

My youngest son, Evan, 6 years old, also wanted to try to slide on the higher rocks, but was not intending to take the same precarious path as his brother. Unfortunately, the river had other plans. Evan was quickly swept into the current and spit right out on the other side. At this time, his brother Zane, 12, had scaled the rocks on the other shore and was already on that side of the river. But these rocks were too high and steep for Evan to climb on, so his only path back to me was through the current.

Zane attempted to help Evan walk across the current, but he realized that the rocks were so slick that he would not be able to gain his footing to cross safely. At this point (after Zane announced that if Evan tried to stepped foot in the current, he would surely die – thanks, Zane!), Evan began to lament that he was stuck there forever. He was pitiful with fear. Zane and I both waded across the current enough to lock hands, but we just didn't have a way to help Evan get across those "fatal" rocks. The situation was becoming a bit serious at this point, as we brainstormed ways to help him across without being swept into the current and into a not-so-friendly-looking rock face ahead.

It was then that my daughter, Katelyn, in a daring feat of bravery, declared that she would save him and flung herself headfirst into the river current! As she quickly got swept into the current, Zane reached down to grab her hand, and she was flung onto the other side of the river with the boys! It was quite a sight to see: my brave daughter, in Superman posture, riding the current to rescue her brother. She took a bit of a hit from a rock in the process, but otherwise made it safely across the current. All the while, I was on the other bank, knowing full well that Evan had the ability to make it across, and encouraging him to be brave.

Long story short, with Katelyn's assistance, we were able to make a human bridge for Evan to get through the current to the other side of the river and back to me. We passed my sweet boy from one arm to the next in order to get him to safety. It was an adventure, to say the least! But more than an adventure, it was a crazy Talley-sized trust exercise. My momma heart swelled as my children banded together to rescue their own. It took teamwork, strength, trust, and faith.

Life is just like that river. There are times when it is calm and seems to be a manageable trickle. It is enjoyable, pretty to look at, and relatively safe. We slide smoothly and wade in the refreshing water. And then there are times when life can swell with unforeseen rains. Stresses and responsibilities start to add up, and our river of life becomes deeper and deeper. Sometimes it may swirl with hardship and pain. It becomes a quick flowing rapid that brings uncertainty and sometimes excitement.

For some, the unfamiliar gushes may incite a sense of thrill and wonder. For some, pure terror. There are many who rise up in the face of life challenges with gusto and courage, anxious to dive into the current and ride it recklessly and fearlessly. There are others who tiptoe to the edge, terrified that the current may sweep them off of their feet and force them into a possibly dangerous situation. Yet we all have one thing in common: We approach the river with the knowledge that we cannot control where it leads, and our presence alone makes us susceptible to its power. Life affords us the same guarantee.

The moment we step foot in the river, we are at the mercy of its current. Sometime life washes over us and we feel helpless to the speed of the rapids. Before we know it, we are headed exactly where we didn't want to go. We become vulnerable to unseen powers and forced to land wherever life deposits us. We are left disoriented and alone. Just like Evan did not intend to head into a dangerous location, he became affected by an unfortunate turn of events. Not one of us could have predicted his outcome, although we did know the risk. And when he entered the river, he assumed that risk.

As Evan found out on the opposite bank, he was unable to gain his footing. The rocks were slippery and impossible for him to cross. So often in my life, I have lost my footing. Unexpected events, or even my own foolish choices, have landed me on the far bank, with no ability to get my feet back under me. I have felt hopeless and scared. It is a terrifying experience.

Sometimes, those around me even add to my panic. When Zane declared to Evan that he was going to succumb to certain death if he tried to cross the river, Evan wailed in terror, "I'm stuck over here forever!" In the same way, I have had negative influences in my life who have spoken words of defeat over my situations. They have caused me to doubt my ability and I want to cry out just like Evan. We cannot allow naysayers in our lives to add to our feelings of hopelessness. Oftentimes, even well-meaning people who are trying to help us actually add to the panic and fear of our situation. It takes discernment on our part to recognize the people in our lives who empower us to get up and find a solution, as opposed to those who are increasing our despair.

Who we want to seek in our lives are the ones who are willing to dive into the current for us! These are the people who do not just tell us what to do from the other side, but literally go head-first into our trials with us. They see our need and will do anything to help us to find a way out. I have been so fortunate in my life to have friends and family who carry the bruises to prove the battering they have taken on for me. They have faced the rocks and braved the current to help me back onto my feet when I didn't have the strength or ability to do it alone.

Surround Yourself

Did you know that there is such a support available to each one of us? When we are adopted into the Family of God, we immediately gain access to the life-saving efforts of other Christians around us. When we find ourselves swept up into the current of life and stranded on the other side, there are believers all around the world who are willing to dive into the current to save us. For this reason, it is essential that we seek them out and surround ourselves with their protection. This may come in the form of your personal family, church family, friends, co-workers, or anyone that is a Godly presence in your life.

If you are in a place right now where you do not have any other believers in your life, I implore you to seek someone out.

Get involved in a local church.

Go where others are seeking God.

Dear Friend, we cannot tackle our trials alone. It takes a strong band of believers to pass us through the Body of Christ until we are able to stand victoriously on dry ground!

God sends amazing people into our lives for just these moments. When we are faced with some of the scariest of life's situations, God creates a team of believers who know we have the courage to do this and who will encourage us from the other side. He sends us those who have gone before us in these trials, who have successfully made it back across the river, and who will wade out into the current to offer a hand to us to help us across. He provides those who are fearless and we gain strength from watching them tackle life recklessly. And I believe that His Daddy heart swells when He sees His children band together to rescue one of their own. It is a crazy, God-sized trust exercise, one that we pray will fill us with strength and faith.

Travel Notes:

Are you connected to a community of believers? If so, who are they? This can come in many forms such as a small group of Christian friends, a church, and Bible study, or your family.

Have you experienced first-hand the benefits of having other believers surrounding you? If so, how?

If you do not have a current community, where can you seek out other believers to help support you?

How can you support other Christians in your community?

10

Sherpas - Mentors

Carry each other's burdens, in this way you will fulfill the law of Christ.
Galatians 6:2[15]

Each year, hundreds of mountaineers attempt to summit the highest peak on planet Earth – Mt. Everest. They train, prepare, purchase high quality equipment, study, and make travel arrangements. Some hikers spend years dreaming and planning. Yet, despite all of their advanced preparations, almost every one of them seeks one additional component to ensure their success at the summit - a Sherpa.

Sherpas are called such according to the regional location of their heritage. Studies have shown that Sherpa people are genetically wired to acclimate to the conditions and high altitudes of Mt. Everest.[16] Their people are familiar with the mountains and have amazing abilities to endure the harsh environment. British mountaineer Kenton Cool, who's climbed Everest 11 times, explains, "The Sherpas are so important. For one, they're the local people, so they know the culture, they know the area, they know the people."[17] This makes them invaluable to go ahead of the foreign mountaineers to provide safe passages and guidance up the mountain. However, their importance extends far beyond their physical ability to climb a mountain. The Sherpas are more than guides; they literally save people's lives.

One thing that stood out to me immediately as I navigated my path to adulthood was my need of a mentor. I quickly realized that I was not qualified to "adult" on my own. I was inexperienced, naïve, ignorant, and scared. This revelation only intensified as a young bride and later as a new mother. I can clearly remember times when I fervently sought out women who possessed more experience than I. I hungered for guidance, wisdom, and assurance. I found out instantly the benefits of surrounding myself with those women who embodied Godly character and strength. Now that I am further in years, I can honestly say that it has been the presence of my mentors that has been one of the largest influences on my life as a wife, mother, daughter, friend, and child of God. I have been blessed with not only guides, but women who have emotionally and mentally saved my life.

Given this, it is easy to see a comparison of the role of a Sherpa to an adventurous mountaineer and the role of a mentor to us as we adventure through our lives. I cannot stress to you enough the importance of finding people in your life who can be your Sherpa.

Our journey through life can be extremely scary and challenging. It is invaluable to have someone beside you who is willing to walk portions of your path with you in order to increase your chance of success. The hikers employ Sherpas to provide them with the experience, knowledge, and skill that they alone do not possess. This is exactly what a Godly friend and mentor will do for you.

The role of a Sherpa is multi-faceted. They are actually quite amazing individuals. They are small in stature, yet full of strength and stamina. They are a beautiful picture of exactly the type of trail mate that we require on our journey. Let's dive a bit deeper into the responsibilities they hold to the hikers they are guiding. I think we can see in them the qualities that fill the men and women who have walked ahead of us in life and are now qualified to offer us their expertise.

They go ahead of us. One of the most important jobs of the Sherpas is that they climb the mountain before any other person in order to navigate the path to the summit. They choose the best route and then proceed to lay ropes and ladders throughout the trail to make sure those routes are safe for the travelers. They are then able to return to Base Camp (the camps set up further down the mountain) and advise climbers of where to hike and what dangers to avoid.

Our mentors have done the same. They typically have already experienced what we are currently going through. They have navigated this part of life and have survived the journey. They come back to us and tell us how to proceed, what path is the safest, and what areas we need to avoid.

A true, Godly guide is not only here to advise us in our journey, but has also taken time, energy, and care to lay safeguards for us along the path. This is the love of one who sincerely has the best interest of others in mind. It is easy for us to go through something and live to tell about it. It is completely different for us to have the forethought to put the needs of others above our own. It would be understandable for the Sherpas of the Himalayan Mountains to traverse Mt Everest, only to return with the bragging rights of conquering it unassisted. Yet that is not their intention. The Sherpas' responsibility to the climbers is to continually climb up and down the mountain, checking the ropes and ladders to ensure that the foreign travelers find safety on the mountain. They put the needs and safety of those they do not know before their very own. Throughout my years, I have been humbled the most by those I have met who have been willing to put the emotional and spiritual needs of others above their own, even as they were clinging to the side of their own mountain.

They shoulder life-giving supplies. The act of climbing Mt. Everest is so rigorous that the majority of foreign hikers cannot possibly carry their own supplies. One of the responsibilities of the hired Sherpa is to carry all of the supplies that their hiking party will need. In large baskets or packs that are mounted on their back and supported by a strap that goes across their forehead, the Sherpa guide is weighed down with food, water, cooking supplies, camping gear, climbing equipment, and most importantly, the essential oxygen that the climber will need.

As I researched the Sherpa culture, I was struck by the ability of these men and women to bear such a load under the treacherous conditions of the ascent. Picture after picture depicted the hiker outfitted with only hiking sticks while the Sherpa walked beside him with a basket on his back almost as large as they are.

Dear Friend, I can count on one hand how many people have walked beside me in life, willing to bear all of the weight of my situation, while all I could manage was to get myself up my mountain. These men and women have shouldered my burden, not with me, but for me. They have carried life-giving supplies that I needed along the way: prayer, encouragement, compassion, kindness, understanding, caring, and love. I cannot stress to you the importance of having a Christian mentor to walk beside you, especially one who knows exactly what you will need for your journey because they have already taken a similar one. If you are at a place in your life when you feel as though you may be losing oxygen – the air is thinning and the path is steep – pray fervently for God to send you someone to help shoulder your load and provide you with the life-giving oxygen that you so desperately need. God is faithful to supply all we need, which often comes in the form of Godly men and women.

They set up camp. During the climb, the Sherpa guides go ahead of the hiking party in order to set up camp for the night. They prepare the tents, put on hot food, and wait to offer much needed rest and replenishment to the climbers. One quality that has affected me the most in the mentors that God has sent into my life has been their ability to do just this. Whatever I am going through, no matter how exhausting or ugly it has been, they have committed to set up camp where I am. They have already gone ahead, and now are able to provide me with what they know I will need to find rest and replenishment in order to keep going.

I wonder how difficult this must be for the Sherpas. After a long day on the mountain, bearing the burden of their hikers, they have to muster the strength to complete this last task of the day. Can you imagine them, braving the cold and the wind to set up the tent, turn on the stove, and cook up a hot meal? Oh, what a sight for sore eyes they must be to the worn and weary mountaineers!

I see this amazing care in my Christian friends who are concerned for my well-being. They long to provide a warm place for me to land at the end of a hard day. They spend the little energy they have left to encourage me to continue on. And what a sight they are! When I feel as though I cannot take another step, there is it! A figurative warm tent and a hot meal! Nourishment for my soul! Comfort for my spirit! Praise God for creating dear people who have the strength to set up camp for others. I promise that God cares enough for you to bring these people into your life. They are sitting by a warm stove, awaiting your arrival, and anxious to fuel you up for your journey.

They ensure the climber's safety. Although all of the above duties are important for a Sherpa guide, the primary goal of a Sherpa is the safety of his hiker. Everything mentioned thus far have been elements that come together to provide the safest experience with the highest chance of success. The Sherpas go above and beyond to aid their foreign hikers, from forging ahead to making a safer passage to clipping hikers to themselves. Regardless of the conditions, the Sherpa places the needs of the hiker above all else.

How fortunate are we when we have someone in our life who fills this position. In our journey through adulthood, recognizing this quality in those around us is of utmost importance. Are you surrounded by people who place priority on your safety and well-being? I will admit that there are people in whom I placed a great deal of trust, only to discover that my safety was farthest from their concern in our relationship. These were hard lessons to learn, but valuable in that I began to seek out those who possessed the characteristic of being protective.

In doing research about how the ropes are secured throughout the climb and instructions on how to safely navigate those ropes, one thought struck me like lightning: *Always ensure that you are clipping in to ropes that have integrity.* There could not be a truer statement as it pertains to our choice of friends. It is vital that we seek out those with strong integrity with which to form relationships that honor God. Friends and loved ones who desire to protect our hearts are priceless.

Proverbs 13:20 encourages us in this: "He who walks with the wise will become wise, but the companion of fools will suffer." Choosing loving, caring, Godly friends will ensure additional security for life's unpredictable terrain.

I love what the article "Mt. Everest the British Story" writes,

> *Another good thing about the Sherpa's is that they can often provide comfort to climbers who are having a hard time. Although very few of them actually speak English, language does not seem to be a barrier when it comes to looking after the climbers. As well as comfort, they can also offer a boost in morale to those who are finding it difficult to want to carry on with the expedition. It can often be hard to get this boost from other climbers, but Sherpas are experienced and have made the climb many times before, so they are going to find it a lot easier than the average climber.*[18]

What a wonderful illustration of what a Godly companion can do for us on our journey, and what we also ought to do for our loved ones. In fact, this is exactly what God calls us to do.

Paul tells Christ followers of the Thessalonian Church, "Therefore encourage one another and build each other up, just as in fact you are doing" (I Thessalonians 5:11 NIV). We are called, as brothers and sisters in Christ, to be observant of those who are finding the trek difficult, to clip them into ourselves, and to give them the boost they need to carry on. In this, although it is important for us to find this quality in a mentor, we must remember that others will be looking to us for this as well.

> *But we who are strong ought to bear with the failings of the weak, and not just please ourselves. (Romans 15:1 NIV)*

They celebrate the summit. I must confess that as I was writing out the roles of the Sherpas with my dear friends and mentors in mind, this one sentence brought me to tears. In the many trials that I have faced in my life, those who are most dear to my heart are the ones who stuck by me through the entire climb and were standing next to me when I finally reached my summit.

We all have our mountains to climb. Life is full of the ups and downs of daily challenges, but sometimes we find ourselves standing at the base of a massive mountain. From our perspective it may seem unsurmountable. Yet we make our slow ascent, step by step. We face treacherous weather, dangerous terrain, and perilous nights. Our mountains are typically life-altering events for us. I do not want to even list what a mountain may look like, for we all have our own to face. Not one will be like the other. I can say that they are the times in our lives when we struggle to visualize ourselves at the daunting summit. It is also a part of our journey to find our true Sherpas – those who have started at the foot of the mountain with us and have trudged step by step with us the entire way to the top. When we do finally reach our mountaintop, they are standing next to us, celebrating as if they had conquered their own summit!

What has struck me about the Nepali Sherpas is their resilience in being present for their hikers at all times. Through the tranquil trails and the precarious passages alike, the guides are there, ensuring that their climber can keep going. In the same way, God knows how much we need the constant presence of Christian guides. Paul urges fellow Christians to "Rejoice with those who rejoice; mourn with those who mourn" (Romans 12:15 NIV). We are called to walk beside one another, taking on the mountain, and then celebrating together when we finally triumph over our trials.

I cannot fail to mention that some of us may not see the top of those mountains. Be it an illness, lifetime ailment, terminal prognosis, physical or mental challenge, broken relationships, or one of many possible figurative Mt. Everests, there are some that will not reach the peak. As Christians we can be assured that there will be a triumphant summit, whether we see it in this lifetime or the next. One of the Psalmists writes,

> One thing I ask of the Lord, this only do I seek: that I will dwell in the house of the Lord all the days of my life, to gaze on the beauty of the Lord and to seek Him in His temple. For in the day of trouble he will keep me safe in his dwelling; he will hide me in the shelter of his sacred tent and set me high upon a rock. Then my head will be exalted above the enemies who surround me; at his sacred tent I will sacrifice with shouts of joy; I will sing and make music to the Lord. (Psalm 27: 4-7)

Whether or not we find worldly success in conquering our mountains, we are confident that the Lord will keep us safe in the journey and will set us high upon the rock, where we will be as joyful as the Mt. Everest mountaineers, and our Godly Sherpas, those sweet loving mentors, will be celebrating right beside us.

Travel Notes:

Based on what you've read about Sherpas, can you identify anyone in your life who has been a Sherpa to you? Who?

What characteristics have you found in friends or mentors that have helped you the most on your journey?

How can you act as a Sherpa to those around you? Is there anyone in particular who God is calling you to mentor or walk beside?

IV

Traveling in Pairs

11

Traveling Solo - Singleness

No one has ever seen God; but if we love one another, God lives in us and his love is made complete in us. I John 4:12[19]

So many young people that I meet have that major question looming over their head: "When will I meet the man/woman of my dreams?"

Finding a spouse seems to be a driving force in our lives, sometimes from a very young age. "Do you have a boyfriend/girlfriend?" is jokingly asked of the youngest children. Social media pages encourage us to define our relationship status in our profiles. We live in a culture that makes having a significant other a status symbol and we question ourselves and others who find themselves single for any length of time. It is a worrisome cultural norm, and one that is probably the most likely to drive us off-course of our path in early adulthood.

As I became a teenager, I can remember how often I would hear the phrase "looking for Mr. Right" – TV, magazine articles, advertisements, music. It seemed everything around me indicated that my primary job as I entered adulthood was to "find" my future mate. As I've aged and God has revealed many truths to me, I have realized that the problem was not in my desire to get married and have a spouse, but in my independent and incessant "search" for him. I can recall many youth church meetings where they explained to us that God had reserved the perfect spouse for us. I remember being taught the importance of purity and keeping myself for my spouse. These messages are vital, and true. God has chosen the perfect one for us, and it is pertinent that we preserve and protect our purity until we meet our spouse.

Yet one aspect of these messages that I seemed to miss was what I was supposed to do while I waited for my spouse. See, it seemed that while the church was telling me that God had the perfect person set aside for me, the world was telling me that I needed to be actively searching out my mate. These messages were conflicting and confusing. What I wish someone had told me was that there was a relationship that I needed to be actively seeking, and that relationship was with God. I needed to keep my eyes on Him, and only Him.

So let's put this into the perspective of our Journey. We have discussed that our Path is unique to each of us and is what will lead us to our ultimate goal of abundant and purposeful life with Him. This path we are on is our lifeline. The Bible tells us that God works all things together for the good of those who love Him (Romans 8:28). Did you hear that, Reader? *All things.* What that means for us travelers is that when we remain in the safety of His path, He allows everything that we encounter to be used to bring good to our lives. There is a condition, however, and that states that He works all things together for the good *of those who love Him.* And loving Him means we are also in obedience to Him. In John 14:15, Jesus tells us "if you love me, then you will keep my commands." And as His Word tells us, obedience is following His will and tuning our hearts into Him. "And this is love: that we walk in obedience to his commands. As you have heard from the beginning, his command is that you walk in love" (2 John 1:6).

Matthew 22:37 reminds us that we are to love God with all of our heart, all of our soul, and all of our mind. When we seek Him first, we are ensuring that our eyes are focused exactly where they need to be so that we can remain in line with where God wants us to go. We need to be seeking His path and doing everything possible to travel confidently on the path He has laid out specifically for us. When we are confident in our path, we can move forward every day, with the assurance that we are walking so closely with God that we immediately recognize any deviance from His route.

Lone Traveler

Although so many of us long for marriage, there will be some who may decide, or God decides for them, to travel their path as a single person. Being single can come in many forms: never married, divorced, widowed. We may be in a season of singleness for many factors, as well. Some will make a conscientious choice to devote themselves to something other than marriage. This may include education, job, travel, family, or ministry. Dating, engagement, and marriage are all wonderful times in life, yet they require a great deal of time and energy. It is understandable to focus on life events that also require our undivided time and energy.

Being single may also be a God thing. Although we may not have chosen to be single at this point in our lives, what if God has other intentions? What if being single is not an accident? What if *God's plan* is you being single, at least for this season? There will be times in our lives when God will ask us to remain where He wants us, even when it will not make sense or goes against what we feel is the desire of our heart. What we must cling to in these times is that God's will is good and loving, and He knows what is best for us. We need to find a place of surrender to be who we are in Christ, whether He chooses a spouse for us or not.

It is in these times that we need to look up to Him and resolve ourselves to stay on His path. Paul says it best in his first letter to the Corinthian church: "Nevertheless, each person should live as a believer in whatever situation the Lord has assigned to them, just as God has called them" (I Corinthians 7:25 NIV). We need to seek contentment in where He has us at this very moment, trusting in Him.

There are times when I get caught up in the "one day." One day I will have more. More love. More money. More stuff. More time. The list can go on and on. One of the biggest "one days" that I believe young people grapple with is "One day I will be married." This appears to be on the hearts of so very many singles. Life seems to hover in limbo, waiting for the day when we meet our future spouse. Almost as if our life will not begin until we meet *The One.* We hinge our decisions and our enjoyment of life on when we will be walking down the aisle.

This is a dangerous place to land, and it happens all too often. If all you are focusing on is being married, you will be stuck in a state of discontent. Do not let your relationship status be your life status. If you have found yourself in this place, I urge you to seek out the One who holds your life in His hands. Ask Him to help you to find contentment in where you are on your journey. For me, when discontent creeps into my life, I have to go straight to the Father and admit that I am unhappy with His plan. Then I have to come to a place of surrender to Him. I have to admit that His way is not my way, but it is a better one. If you are in this place of discontentment with your relationship status, you may need to stop seeking a person to make you happy or whole. Let Jesus fulfill these things for you.

When we finally come to reconcile that we know we are where God wants us to be, we will be able to make forward progress, grounded in contentment, which in turn will bring us joy in the journey. Trusting that God longs to please us and thrill us, we can now enjoy the path. When we are constantly looking around for a mate, we will most likely take our focus off of the current scenery. We may be straining to peer ahead, or possibly we are stuck looking behind at what we thought should have been. Either way, our eyes are straying from His path and what He longs for us to experience in the moment.

I have been guilty of doing just that when my family and I go hiking. I often have a set destination, which is usually a waterfall. I love seeking out waterfalls. They are the driving force behind my hikes. Unfortunately, in my crazy waterfall obsession, I often miss the treasures along the way. My children, on the other hand, are wonderful at finding beauty in the smallest places on the trail. My second son, Zane, for instance, loves to photograph any flower, twig, leaf, mushroom, grass, and rock on the path. He will insist on stopping every few feet to snap an artistic interpretation of an ordinary piece of nature. I will have to admit that this habit of his has caused this mama some serious anxiety. Ashamedly, I have hurried him along in

111

an attempt to stay on my schedule. Oh, how guilty I felt after one look at his stunning pictures! He has a true gift of finding beauty in the most humble places. He shows me what I have missed by focusing too intently on the end result.

When we are focused on Him, our eyes on *His* path, we may see some amazing sights! Just seek God. Let Him direct your path. Psalm 37:4 urges us to "Delight in the Lord and He will give you the desires of your heart." God longs to give us the desires of our heart, but sometimes our desires are not in line with His will. In these cases, we need to seek *His* heart, for what if, as we come closer to Him, His desires actually *become* our desires? What if we stick so faithfully to His Path that we have no chance of getting lost, or falling out of His will? We find confidence in His calling on our lives when we refuse to stray from the trail that He has set before us. And that trail may very well lead us into singleness, maybe for a season or possibly for the entire journey. Singleness is not something to fix. Use this season to have undivided devotion to Jesus. Live sold out to Him. Become "all in" and then relax and take in the sights. They are sure to be spectacular!

Forging the Path Alone, But Not Really

Singleness is a very difficult place for many people to camp, but it is a possibility that must be entertained. Marriage seems to be the societal life goal, yet it truly isn't a Biblical one. Dr. Keith Shorter addresses this in his sermon entitled "Single, but Not Alone,"

> *Promising marriage is not Biblical. There was never someone promised to everyone in the Bible. Paul is a great example of someone who was called to live his life unmarried. His devotion to spreading the Word of God was so that marriage could have very possibly hindered his mission, yet Paul was single his whole life.*

Paul writes to the church of Corinth regarding this very thing. "I wish that all of you were as I am [unmarried]. But each of you has your own gift from God; one has this gift, another has that. Now to the unmarried and the widows I say: It is good for them to stay unmarried, as I do. But if they cannot control themselves, they should marry, for it is better to marry than to burn with passion" (I Corinthians 7:7-8).

Paul reiterates what we have been unpacking throughout this book: God has equipped us each with a unique set of gifts. We will read later about how, for those of us who choose to marry, we will find that our partners possess qualities that complement our gifts and talents. Yet that does not undermine the pack-full of resources that He has bestowed upon those who are single. God has given all of us the ability to successfully navigate our path to Him. For some, that journey will involve a partner who is our spouse. However, I will argue that this does not mean that the person who is unmarried will walk their path alone.

Our lives are full of people who cross our path daily, and every one of them brings something to our journey. God knows precisely who we need along our way, and a spouse is not the only one who can fulfill this. Friends and family will come beside us and travel step by step with us. They will enjoy the beautiful views with us, as well as help us traverse obstacles in our path. They will bring with them the skills, gifts, and blessings that will aid us in our adventures. Please do not ever believe that someone needs a spouse in order to be fulfilled or be fooled into thinking that marriage equals a successful life. Having a spouse along our journey is a blessing, but it is not vital to walk a beautifully full, thrilling, meaningful journey.

Travel Notes:

What are your feelings about your current relationship status?

If you are single, are you content in where God has you at this time? Why or why not?

Is there something in your life - education, career, family, ministry - that God may be calling you to focus on? If so, what is it and where can you see God working?

Are you willing to accept God's timing and plan for your relationships? Why or why not? Pray to God for wisdom, guidance, and peace in where He has you right now.

12

Point of Convergence - Marriage

Therefore what God has joined together, let no one separate. Mark 10:9[20]

Being confidently rooted in God is crucial for our journey to marriage. For at the same time that we are headed in a forward direction on our own path, God has our future mate on a path of his or her own. As we are both moving toward Him, He is lovingly moving us toward each other. And then, in His timing, He thrills us with His divine Point of Convergence: the point when our separate paths unite and we begin, not a new journey, but a new phase of our journeys.

During this phase, we become a team with our spouse, and from this point forward, we have the honor of sharing every intimate step with him or her. Understanding the union of our paths is critical. It is strictly by the convergence of our individual paths that we will find success together. Our paths have to merge into one another, not overtake the other.

Have you ever seen the MERGE road sign? It clearly shows two roads becoming one. That's what we are looking for in a marriage. But what we need to understand is that for us to merge with one another, we must first meet some criteria.

1. *We need to be traveling on our own path first.* Our solo journey to our God-ordained destination is our first and foremost priority. We need to set our GPS and then be willing to follow His direction unabashedly. We need to be in tune with him and unwilling to veer from His guidance. We need to be walking so closely to Him that we

do not even see the world's distractions swirling around us. "Seek first His kingdom and His righteousness, and all of these things will be given to you as well" (Matthew 6:33 NIV). God desires for us to run after Him. He longs for our attention above all others. And when our eyes are looking nowhere but on Him, He can do His best work because we are not letting our earthly agendas get in His way. An important note about merging is that cars begin in their independent lanes before joining with the other. The only way to properly merge with our intended spouse is to be traveling in our own lane and moving in the direction that God has intended for us.

2. *We need to be traveling in the same direction.* If you notice the Merge road sign, you will note one thing: the traffic on each road is flowing in the same direction. You will not see northbound cars merging with southbound. That would result in disaster. There would be collisions and destruction of mass proportions. We can say the same about marriage. We must be traveling in the same direction of our intended spouse; and as Christians that direction is toward eternal life with Jesus. In 2 Corinthians 6:14 Paul urges Christians to seek out other believers in marriage, "Do not be yoked together with unbelievers. For what do righteousness and wickedness have in common? Or what fellowship can light have with darkness?"

I know that these words sound harsh, especially when we find someone who sets our heart pumping, but they are not to be taken lightly. Phylicia Masonheimer writes in her article "Why Being Unequally Yoked is More Dangerous than You Think,"

> *If Christ is truly King of our lives, our most intimate selves should be submitted to His influence. How then can we unite a Spirit-led soul to one in rebellion against God? This rubs people the wrong way, because no matter how respectful, sweet, or 'loving' an unbelieving partner is, he is at odds with Christ – he is in rebellion.*

But if we call ourselves Christians, we're saying we believe the Bible is our final authority. The Bible says that all have sinned and fallen short of the glory of God and that without Christ we are '[unresponsive] in our transgressions', conformed to the world, 'living by the cravings of our flesh' and 'by nature, children of wrath'. (Eph. 2:1-3) This is who we are without Jesus. This is who everyone is apart from Christ.[21]

God is very specific regarding this command (2 Cor 6:14). It is vital as a believer to allow only those on our path who have the same destination. Therefore, our prayer as a single person should be that our intended spouse is also seeking God closely and obediently staying in His path. The world is going to tell you that this doesn't matter. But, Young Friend, God tells you that it does. We may think it a burden to wait on God for our Divine Point of Convergence. We may become frustrated and impatient. We may feel as though God has forgotten about us. But He has not. He is waiting. Waiting for the perfect moment when our paths will merge. Take heart in what Masonheimer writes,

Being equally yoked is not meant to inhibit our dating lives. Rather, it is a command designed for protection and honor. Being unequally yoked is more dangerous than you think – and waiting for someone with whom you share the same spiritual heritage is far more rewarding than many believe.

To be yoked is by Meriam-Webster definition "a wooden bar or frame by which two draft animals (such as oxen) are joined at the head or neck for working together."[22] The relationship between the oxen would be completely ineffective if they were facing opposite directions. Inasmuch, I am pretty sure that if there were a wooden frame attached to the shoulders of you and your mate, it would be impossible for you to travel in separate directions. You would be at a standstill.

In the illustration given us by Paul in 2 Corinthians, God gives us a clear picture as to the importance of us yoking ourselves with believers. He makes this command, not to be exclusive, but to promote our best interest and our highest chance of success in our marriage journey. God knows how difficult our path may be, which is why He designed us to not have to carry the load alone. He intended for us to have a helpmate, even from the first. "The Lord God said, 'It is not good for the man to be alone. I will make a helper for him'" (Genesis 2:18).

Another definition of yoke that I love is "a frame fitted to a person's shoulders to carry a load in two equal portions" (Miriam-Webster). Two equal portions. Sharing the load. I love this image. As part of a married team for 20 years, I can tell you how reassuring it has been to have my husband walking beside me to share the load of life. Without him shouldering his portion of life's heaviness, I would have surely been crushed beneath the weight of it. Under the blessing of God, we have been able to merge beautifully. My husband and I are truly each other's helpmate. We are a team, tackling life shoulder to shoulder. Neither is ahead of the other, but connected on the same level. I have seen in full color how God uses a Christian marriage to be a powerhouse for Him. He longs to bless each of us the same. Following His command ensures that power found in His way. [Sidenote for singles: Jesus also uses the illustration of being yoked as being yoked to Him so that He may share our load. Do not dismiss the ability of Christ to be a beautiful life partner for us.]

3. *You must be prepared for oncoming traffic.* At the stage in our lives when marriage becomes a real option is when we need to be the most in tune to who God wants to bring into our lives. All throughout your life, God is preparing your heart as well as your spouse's for your intended convergence. Our prayers and intentions need to be so focused on Him, that when He does bring our beloved into our lives, we will have no doubt that he/she has been ordained for us by God. One of the concerns that I frequently hear is "how will I know if the person I fall in love with is the one God intends for me?" You will know because you have spent time with the Father and have prepared your heart for who He desires for you.

My husband and I are Clemson University alum. We love our Tigers. Dabo Swinney, the coach that led our team to the National Championship in 2016, initiated a motto with his team: "All In" became plastered on t-shirts, posters, practically the entire town. Dabo encouraged his players to be "All In" for their team, for the win, for each other. This is a great reminder for us too. We need to be "All In" for Jesus. No matter the time in our lives, we need to be completely and utterly devoted to learning, praying, and soaking up Jesus; however, this is especially important during this time that God is preparing your heart for marriage. When we are not tuned in to Him, it is easy for us to not recognize the one God intends for us. We are not prepared for the oncoming traffic. We become overwhelmed by the dating world and become anxious and worried about our future.

When I was learning to drive, I hated when my lane merged with another. The road sign itself evoked a cold sweat. I would tense my shoulders, tighten my grip on the wheel, and hold my breath when those merging cars were approaching. It was overwhelming for me. I believe marriage can create this same anxiety. We worry about who God will bring and how we will know. We worry that we will marry the wrong person and we will end in divorce. We worry that we will miss Mr. or Mrs. Right. Yet when we are "all in" for God, we allow Him to ease our anxiety. We rest in confidence that we are so zeroed in on God that we will clearly recognize our Divine Convergence.

I once read that a person trained to recognize fraudulent money never studies the fake ones. They only study the real deal. They do this in order that they will be so familiar with what is right that they will immediately recognize what is wrong. We also need to be this way. We need to study His way so that any person who is not in God's will stands out clearly to us. We need to have such an intimate relationship with our Father that His will is the only one that we recognize. He is the real deal, and whoever He brings into our lives will be as well.

Just as when we are preparing to merge our vehicles into a lane with another, it is crucial that we not only look for what is approaching, but that we are also keeping our eyes focused on our own destination. Merging our lives together with someone is exhilarating. Do not be sidetracked by what is ahead or what is coming from behind. Set yourself on God's route and then enjoy the ride as He works to orchestrate a blessed point of convergence that will lead to a lifelong journey together with your spouse.

Travel Notes:

Where do you see yourself on your path in regards to relationships? Are you content with traveling solo? Have you been seeking out someone to start a relationship with? Are you in a relationship that is moving towards marriage? Are you newly married?

Regardless of the above, where are you in your personal path with God?

Does your answer to the second question affect your answer to the first? If so, how?

What benefits do you see in ensuring that we are focused in on God's direction before we merge our paths with another person?

Do you need to make any changes in order to accomplish this? If so, what?

13

Combining Resources - Teamwork

Two are better than one, because they have a good return for their labor: If either of them falls down, one can help the other up. Ecclesiastes 4:9a[23]

As our journey with our beloved begins, we start to unwrap wonderful characteristics about each other. We learn what they love, what they are good at, and what makes them unique. We become enamored by their strengths and starry eyed by their character. And we also learn about what they do not like, what they do poorly, and what makes them different from us. We find out that they have weaknesses and flaws in their character. All of this is what makes the early stages of a relationship exciting. We are discovering everything we can about our partner in an attempt to understand who he/she is and what our life will look like together. This time is usually full of pleasant surprises and thrilling discoveries. It also sometimes brings with it slight disappointments. These often do not come until the thrill of a new relationship wears off a bit, but they are there all the same. All of these things that you are discovering are necessary pieces of information that will be vital throughout your journey.

Jumanji

My children and I recently watched the movie *Jumanji: Welcome to the Jungle,* about four high school kids who discover an old video game console and are drawn into the game's jungle setting, literally becoming the adult avatars they choose. The teenagers embark on a dangerous adventure to beat the game and return to reality. What I loved in the movie is that when they first find themselves inside of the video game and have chosen their avatars, they are given a list of qualities of those avatars' strengths, weaknesses, characteristics, etc. These qualities pop up on a screen for them to see. Throughout their adventure, they pull from their knowledge of these characteristics in order to work together to defeat the game. They take a resource inventory on their entire team and then apply this knowledge as challenges arise.

I will be honest; there were many times when I was single that I wished a screen would pop up to alert me of the strengths/weaknesses of the gentleman I was dating. Wouldn't it be easy if those characteristics were so easily available to us at the beginning of our adventure with our intended spouse? For example, my husband's pop up may have looked something like this: Strengths – remains calm in stressful situations; Weakness – cannot locate the dishwasher. In fairness, mine would look like this: Strengths – able to handle high amounts of chaos; Weakness – forgets to cook dinner.

All kidding aside, it takes a lot of work to discover what each of us brings into a relationship. Yet we all possess a unique set of qualities that will aid or deter our journey together. It takes a great deal of discernment to assess the qualities of our spouse or future spouse and then to have the ability to use them to work together.

If you are just now beginning a new relationship, it is not as easy to see the entire spectrum of your partner's qualities. We tend to look through rose-colored glasses and see only the good things. This is necessary in order for us to be swept away by our beloved. If we saw the unattractive qualities right away, we would never get married! But those unattractive tendencies do come and we have to be prepared for them.

I often remind others that our partners are putting their best foot forward while trying to woo us. When we are dating, we most likely see the best of the other person. This is not to say that our spouse cannot get better – we all make improvements with time – but this is the time that our partner is most committed to impressing us.

As we date, we need to keep in mind that if there are qualities that we feel need to change for us to be happy with him/her, we may want to rethink our future together. We must be satisfied and happy with exactly who our partner is at the time we are dating. So many enter marriage with the thought that "they will get better" or "if they love me, they will change." Sometimes they do, but what if they don't?

We need to make sure that we can accept our spouse for who they are when they stand at the altar beside us. I love that we are continual works in progress, and I pray that through the past 20 years I have grown into a better version of who my husband married; however, I am beyond thankful that Chris accepted me for who I was the day he married me and has never expected any more from me. That is not an easy thing to do. I am also thankful that my mother-in-law reminded me as a young bride that "I knew what I signed up for."

There were several times in the early days of marriage when the glasses didn't seem so rosy anymore and the disappointment of finding chinks in my knight's armor set in, that I had to cling to those words. I knew what I signed up for. I took this man – flaws and all – and promised to be with him. And there has been a gentle assurance for the past 20 years that he is exactly who I need beside me. He is not perfect, but he is perfect for me. And how can I be so sure of this?

It is the assurance that comes from placing my life in the hands of the Father. The confidence in walking in His path and trusting that the one He chose to merge my life with is the one who is perfectly equipped to go on this adventure with me. Years later, I can clearly see our "pop ups." Our strengths, weaknesses, and characteristics may seem crazy to anyone else, but they make perfect sense to us. They are exactly what we have needed to successfully navigate our journey so far. As in the game of *Jumanji*, life has thrown challenges and obstacles our way, yet we have found that we each possess the precise qualities needed for victory.

So That's What That Was For!

Can you remember when we took a resource inventory of that backpack God has gifted each of us? Let us recollect that the items that God has placed in our pack are the exact tools that we need to navigate our journey through life. And each of us has a very unique set of resources that have been specifically selected by God Himself for us individually. What an honor to know that God took the time, energy, and love to pack our bags with such care and concern.

Well, Friend, God packed one for our spouse one too. And his/her backpack will be full of many things that are similar to yours, yet many things that will be dramatically different. The resources that our partner possesses will define what he/she brings into the marriage. This is an important concept to understand, for it will allow you to find value in your partner. We need to acknowledge that our spouse will also come into our marriage with a unique set of resources, some that we may appreciate right away, and some that may take us years to uncover the value. Yet each one is designed to perfectly compliment what is in our pack.

In our youth, we may have looked in our pack and seen items that just did not make sense. For example, when I looked in my own figurative pack, I may have found a climbing harness. What is the purpose of this piece of equipment? Well, in my years as an instructor of high ropes courses, I can tell you that a harness is essential for survival. It holds the climber up and supports him/her. It was the very first gear we would inspect before we took to the trees. And although most every other piece of equipment comes with a backup in case of a malfunction, a harness most often does not – leaving it to be an item that requires constant inspection and care. The integrity of the harness, the wear and tear, and its strength all contribute to its effectiveness as a life-saving tool.

This figurative harness translates perfectly into a character trait that I possess. I am a supporter. I have spent my entire life holding others up. God has given me the gift of encouragement and fortitude. In my family, that equates to me being the one who drives our energy and directs our days. I am the one with the crazy ideas and the boldness to follow through on them. I am the emotional support for my husband and my children. I am the risk taker and the adventurer, always pushing us to new heights. And my friends will testify that God puts my family and my children deep into my heart. I am also called to reach out to others and encourage them and find ways to support them in their own endeavors. Yet this trait often leaves me with extra wear and tear. I cannot find the strength alone but find great strength from my relationship with Jesus. In Him, I love to feel my legs dangle in the freedom His strength gives me. I am a harness.

Now, if I am honest with you, I will admit that in my figurative pack I most definitely lack a rope, a basic item that one would think any great adventurer would possess. But you see, the function of a rope is for protection from a fall or to enhance movement either up or down. Considering that I am spontaneous, and frankly, a bit careless by nature, I would offer that I do not often think about laying the ropes before I begin on an adventure. I fail think about what needs to be done in order to protect myself from falling. In life, this means that I end up taking risks without ensuring a network of safety. I throw myself into holding others up, despite the fraying on my soul. My confidence in what I want to accomplish – aka in my harness – is such that I fail to remember to bring with me the one item that will keep me from falling to an untimely death. A rope is vital. It allows us to takes those risks with the confidence of safety.

In self-evaluation as a young person, overconfidence in my harness (support) and my lack of rope (protection) led to some costly life choices. As I look back, I realize that I often got banged up by some poor, spontaneous decisions. It was not until I met Chris that I knew that I had been lacking a vital piece of equipment for my emotional survival. I was missing my rope.

Wikipedia defines a rope as being designed to absorb the energy of a falling climber by reducing the maximum force experienced by the climber.[24] This is exactly what Chris brought into my life. He became my security. His strength, caution, and protection allow me to step out over the cliff of life's challenges with the confidence that he will not let me fall. He holds my safety as a high priority. Another purpose of a rope is to act as an anchor. Wow! That perfectly describes what my spouse is to me. He is my anchor. In all of my wild passions of life - my ideas, my excitements, my failures - he is there to hold me secure. He keeps me anchored by his calm, logical character.

What I had to discover through time is that God packed my backpack with certain resources that are the perfect complement to what is in Chris's pack. Just as I have benefited from the ability of my husband to hold fast to me and get us through the most precarious obstacles, he has also benefited from my encouragement, support, and fearlessness. I bring to our marriage the harnesses that not only allow us to take risks, but also support us through the times when we have been left to scale gigantic rock faces.

When we paired together our talents, gifts, and God-given resources, we understood why God chose to bless us with them. It is so very important that we see our spouse as the valuable companion to our personal traits. We will so often focus on the differences between us and our spouse, but taking another look at them through the eyes of the Father will increase your love and appreciation for the one who He uniquely designed just for you. Whether we are entering into a relationship, or we have been walking beside our partner for decades, taking a resource inventory allows us to recognize what he/she has brought along and trust that both of our packs are full of resources to strengthen and enhance our journey together. Trust in Him, grab each other's hand, and get ready to have the adventure of a lifetime!

Travel Notes:

Imagine yourself in the game of Jumanji. What strengths, weaknesses, or unique characteristics would pop up for you?

How might these characteristics benefit your future or current spouse?

If you are in a relationship, are there things about your mate that you feel need to change? If so, will you be able to have a successful relationship even if they never do?

What strengths or unique traits does your partner bring to your relationship? How do they complement your traits?

If you are not in a relationship, what traits do you hope to find in a future spouse that will complement your own?

14

A Kayak in the Desert - Differences

I appeal to you, brothers and sisters, in the name of our Lord Christ Jesus, that all of you agree with one another in what you say and that there be no divisions among you, but that you be perfectly united in mind and thought.
I Corinthians 1:10[25]

As we talked about what God has equipped us with in our backpack, and how, if He ordains us to marry, many of those items will complement those of our spouse. However; when we travel the trail with another person, we sometimes find that we bring items along our journey that may end up hindering our progress instead of helping it. We sometimes feel as though we need to supplement what God has given us with what we believe we ought to bring along the journey. Although our intentions are to help, this most often holds us back in a relationship.

I had a friend in college who married a young man. Both of them brought to the marriage battle wounds and scars. Having survived a torrid past, her inability to recognize her own worth left her feeling less than adequate to be the wife that her husband deserved. She saw him as strong and capable and many things that she was not. This feeling in turn caused her to seek ways to compensate for what she perceived as her weakness.

There are times in your journey when you may feel inadequate in a situation. Maybe it is feeling inferior to a spouse or a family member or in a job. So you look around for the most impressive, largest item you can find to prove to others that you are capable and strong. Ah-ha, a kayak! That is impressive. Large. Shiny. Colorful. You shoulder this massive kayak and start walking. Whew, this thing is heavy! No worries, you can drag it. This portion of your path is in the desert; that's easy terrain. As the kayak drags behind you, it leaves a cloud of dust to mark the trail.

You begin strong, but soon begin to weary. It is hot. You are tired. And frankly, you may even begin to wonder if this big thing is worth its weight. But you are determined. You are sure that this is still a great idea. Why wouldn't it be? You are showing others how strong you are to handle such a massive load. And it seems that other people you see are also carrying kayaks; therefore, this must be a valuable resource for your journey.

What you fail to see is that those other travelers you see with their kayaks have swift waters up ahead. They will need to carry such a weighty burden now in order to navigate what life will bring them down the trail. However, let us not mistake what they need with what we *think* we need. Let us not look to what others are bringing into their relationships and make assumptions as to what we actually need for ours.

When we compare our abilities with those around us, we will find ourselves lacking almost every time. This results in us feeling inadequate to match the skills of those on our path with us. Let me be clear: God has equipped you perfectly. Trusting in Him to work you and your relationships together for His purpose is a crucial step to a successful journey.

A Little Help Here!

A common trap that we fall into is the martyr trap. "I've been dragging this kayak all this way, and he/she has not once offered to help carry it." Or you may even feel as though your spouse, friend, child, coworker, etc. is sitting in the kayak, allowing you to drag him/her through your journey. When we are fearful of inadequacies, we often try to take on things that are much too big for us in order to overcompensate for what we conceive as our weakness. This inability to recognize the tools that the Maker has equipped us with and the actions of choosing our own resources instead, is a sinful behavior. God doesn't make mistakes. He didn't put the wrong tools in our pack. Whether we have faith in their effectiveness or not, our job as a Christian is to trust in the One who equipped us.

When we fail to value our gifts and talents in a relationship, we panic and then feel the need to prove that we have the ability to have what we perceive as the "right stuff." That leads to us looking around at what other people possess, longing for their gifts and convincing ourselves that what they have is exactly what we need. There is so much danger in this situation, and the consequences can be severe:

1. *We collapse in exhaustion.* Dragging a kayak through the desert is tough stuff. There is only so long that we can continue to search for water. With the sun beating down on us, we weary quickly. We slow down to almost a crawl. We become dirty, and sweaty, and defeated. We have limited ability to shoulder such a burden in life. When we pick up extra weight that was never intended for us to bear, it can literally bring us to our knees. God has purposefully designed us to endure *our* path, no matter the challenges. But we cannot do it by bearing additional weight unnecessarily.

2. *We hinder our progress.* God has set our life to His pace. When we are tuned into Him and trust in His provisions, we are able to keep up the pace He intended for us. But when we decide that we need more than He has provided, we make executive decisions to carry items with us that will soon alter that pace. It may be a job, a friendship, an addiction, or a sin that hinders our progress. It may not stop us in our path, but it will cost us in the end.

3. *We become resentful.* As mentioned above, soon you begin to realize that your trail mate has little intention of helping you haul this boat through the sand. As you walk, you become irritated. You are working hard to bring along this life-saving piece of equipment, and no one is appreciating your effort. Better yet, they aren't even offering to lighten your load. They could at least grab an end, right? But chances are they have seen your foolishness in bringing the boat along. It is seen as unnecessary. When we attempt to be more than we are, we often come across looking foolish. In our effort to prove our strength and ability, we possibly create more doubt and confusion about us. Our judgment is questioned. Others' trust in our competence falters.

We create exactly the opposite of what we hope to achieve – we do not fool anyone by our attempted feats of strength.

How many kayaks have I dragged through the desert? Ah, too many to count, I would imagine. When I have failed to trust in God's provision, when I have valued other people's gifts above my own, when I have doubted my ability, when I have brought stubbornness and pride into a relationship, I start dragging a kayak.

We drag kayaks when we demand that our way is the best way, and when we insist that those on our journey should do everything in their power to make our way work. We start resenting that they aren't helping to shoulder the load, and even accuse them of catching a free ride. All of these circumstances remind us that our fleshly capabilities are limited. For many, that is scary. It is hard to admit that we may not have the answers, or the strength, or the knowledge to handle what lies ahead. And that fear initiates a desire in us to take matters into our own hands.

Dear Reader, God never desires this because he knows that you are never *not* enough. He has given you every gift, talent, and resource that He needs you to have to not only complete your journey, but also to assist those who walk alongside of you. We need only to trust in His ability to see the path ahead and to have confidence that He has equipped us as necessary. Put down the kayak, feel the freedom of lightening your load, and carry on with faith in His provision.

Travel Notes:

Are there character traits that you wish you possessed?

Are you dragging a kayak? If so, what does it represent in your life?

What has been the consequence of adding unnecessary burdens in your life?

How can you begin to trust God more for the resources He has given you, instead of trying to search out traits and characteristics you do not need?

V

Trail Hazards

15

Thieves and Robbers - Spiritual Attacks

But the Lord is faithful, and He will strengthen you and protect you from the evil one. 2 Thessalonians 3:3[26]

I have been a Christian since I was 5 years old. My faith and trust in my loving God has been unwavering, for He has been faithful to me.

Yet even in the security of my trust in Him, I have experienced times when I have taken my eyes off of Him and His ways. I have allowed the world to woo me into believing that there are better views if only I veer off His path for just a little while.

I can tell you, Sweet Reader, that most often my decisions have not been ones of outright disobedience to Him, but more of subtle detours that I thought would not affect my final destination - a desire for a more scenic route, so to speak. I can say with confidence that every missed step has reminded me that there are no self-guided detours in *His* path. He is fully aware of every bump and turn in my life, and He has planned accordingly. It is when I have been overly confident in my own ability to navigate my journey that I have encountered preventable trail hazards. To be sure, I have encountered my fair share of stumbles and pitfalls along my journey. You see, there have been times in my life when I have left myself open to unnecessary dangers. In search of a better view, I have allowed myself to selfishly veer from His path, and I have regrettably found myself looking straight into the face of misfortune.

Although we oftentimes do not intend to run into such trouble, when we take our eyes off of His way, we leave ourselves vulnerable to the dangers that lie ahead. Trail hazards present themselves in many forms, some more obvious than others. We need to prepare ourselves to recognize these hazards so that we will know how to respond when we run into them. And we *will* run into them, that is a given. No human, including Jesus Himself, has been immune to the attacks of the flesh. We all will face a time when we must make a conscious choice to remain on God's path, even when the pull of sin and doubt is strong. The Bible is full of warnings; let us take a look at a few of the most common trail hazards we may stumble upon.

Kill, Steal, and Destroy

It was mentioned in an earlier chapter that one consequence of leaving the secure path provided to us by our loving Father is that we may run into unfriendly travelers. When we deviate from His path, we leave ourselves susceptible to the attacks of thieves and robbers. Their only goal is to take from us and leave us stranded. Satan is no different. Just as Jesus has a goal for our lives, Satan also has a goal for our lives.

Remember that Satan is in the business of lies and destruction, and we know that he will use any means to further his endeavors. Satan has a goal for your life: to kill, steal, and destroy. He never comes to help you, only to hurt you. He never has your best interest in mind. He only comes for his own purpose. He always comes to take from you. Sounds a bit like a thief, doesn't it? Have you ever met a thief that takes your well-being into consideration? Of course not. In the same way, you can be sure that Satan has never and will never have consideration for your well-being.

There was a time in the life of our family when one of my children was aggressively under attack from Satan. He found a foothold in this child and caused torment both emotionally and spiritually. As soon as we discovered the problem, addressed it, and were able to find victory over it, he found another foothold. This one was bigger and the stakes were higher. Once again, when we discovered the problem and resolved it, he found yet another foothold. Let it be known: Satan is relentless. He will not let go easily. He is very good at putting up a fight. Do not ever underestimate his persistence. You are important to him and he will do everything he can to pull you as far away from the presence of God as possible.

The battle for my child was fierce and downright terrifying. We could see before our very eyes the intensity of a spiritual battle. We witnessed a thief in the night, prowling for a young child's soul. Many people are hesitant to speak of Satan and his powers. I believe we do not address it enough in the Christian community. He is real and he is powerful. However, he is not as powerful as our Savior! Although Satan will try his best to gain victories over our souls, we know that in the end, we have One who will be victorious! Yet that does not diminish his efforts nor our need to be vigilant of his prowlings. He would like nothing more than to steal your testimony for Christ. Hiker beware! There is a thief on the prowl and our only defense is to rely upon the One who we know can defeat even the most aggressive attacks. Be brave, we have a great Protector among us.

The Shepherd

There are many illustrations of Jesus's protection on our lives found throughout the Bible, but I would venture that none is quite so utilized as the image of Christ as our Shepherd. In Old and New Testament alike, Jesus is referred to as the Good Shepherd, faithfully attending and guarding his flock, meaning the Church (Christians). One illustration that I love is when Jesus refers to himself as the gatekeeper. In Jesus' time, shepherds would drive their sheep into a round rock-walled pen that had an opening for the sheep to enter. During the night, the shepherd would lay in the opening of the pen so that he would know if anyone or anything was threatening his flock. Jesus uses this metaphor clearly in the Gospel of John.

> *Very truly I tell you, I am the gate for the sheep. All who have come before me are thieves and robbers, but the sheep have not listened to them. I am the gate; whoever enters through me will be saved. They will come in and go out, and find pasture. The thief comes to kill and destroy; I have come that they may have life, and have it to the full. I am the good shepherd. The good shepherd lays down his life for his sheep. (John 10:7-11 NIV)*

Jesus knows that Satan is sneaky and that he loves to creep into our lives undetected in order to bring havoc and destruction. Jesus warns us that Satan will sneak people into our lives for the sole purpose of harming us. "Very truly I tell you Pharisees, anyone who does not enter the sheep pen by the gate, but climbs in by some other way, is a thief and a robber" (John 10:1 NIV). It is essential that we make ourselves aware of the schemes of the devil in order to guard ourselves from his hurtful plans. Never underestimate the lengths that Satan will go to in order to bring us down, using negative influences like unhealthy relationships, tragic events, disappointments, or personal failures.

Don't Be Caught Off Guard

One of the most important defenses that any person can have against a physical attack is being aware of their surroundings. It is critical to know who is around us and what our risks are at all times, especially when we find ourselves in a dangerous situation. An article I read years ago about how to fend off an attack gave the illustration of what to do if you find yourself in an empty parking garage with a potentially dangerous stranger. The article recommended making eye contact with him, speaking to him, and making him aware that you notice him and are paying attention. This takes away his element of surprise. I believe this same defense tactic should be used in dealing with Satan. We need to recognize his tactics, look him in the eye and make him aware that we know what he is up to. He needs to know that we are paying attention and will not be taken off guard. We need to take away his element of surprise.

This is why Jesus warns us of the thieves and robbers. Notice that He does not say that they come barging in to steal the sheep. No, He tells us that they do not use the gate, but sneak in another way. In the same way, He is warning us of those in our lives who are under the influence of the devil, who do not come to us in righteousness of God,

143

but instead sneak into our lives by the back door.

Jesus also gives us positive direction: He tells us who we do need to seek out.

> *The one who enters by the gate is the shepherd of the sheep. The gatekeeper opens the gate for him, and the sheep listen to his voice. He calls his own sheep by name and leads them out. When he has brought out all his own, he goes on ahead of them, and his sheep follow him because they know his voice. But they will never follow a stranger; in fact, they will run away from him because they do not recognize a stranger's voice.* (John 10:1-6 NIV)

We need to know the Shepherd's voice in order to recognize it. It is by hearing, listening to, and following the One who is watching out for our best interests that we find security and peace. Just as the sheep benefit most by learning the voice of their shepherd and following only his, we also need to follow only God's voice in our lives. Do not be fooled by the multitude of voices that are telling you where the world wants you to go. Remember what the goal of the thief is: to take and destroy. We want to look to the One who is the giver of life. If we do not recognize His voice, how will we ever know that we are on the right path? We will be fooled and that will lead us directly into danger, "Whoever walks in integrity walks securely; but whoever takes crooked paths will be found out" (Proverbs 10:9 NIV). Eventually, the schemes of the devil will be unearthed. There will come a day when all creation will see the fallacy of his promises, and the validity of Christ's: "Know that the LORD, he is God! It is He who made us, and we are his; we are his people, and the sheep of his pasture" (Psalm 100:4 NIV).

Alone in the Dark

The times that we are most susceptible to attacks are when we find ourselves alone and in the dark. Think about how often physical attacks occur at night. For our own safety, we are always advised to avoid being alone when possible; I even advise my children to "have a buddy" with them at all times.

It is because being alone and in the dark leaves us vulnerable. It allows us to feel lost, unaware of our surroundings, and open to attack. Yet as Christians, we are never truly alone. Although life often brings us feelings that we are abandoned and vulnerable, we are in a constant presence of the Lord. I will say it again, we are never alone.

I want to share with you words from my dear young friend, Hannah, who found herself in just such a state.

> Last night at midnight I suddenly realized I didn't know where I was. I was following the GPS home not knowing I was taking a different way than when I had come. My phone was saying I was on my way home, but to me, I was just alone in the dark. It's an accurate analogy of this messy season I'm in. It's a funny thing knowing where you're going but having no idea where you are. So often I find the road looks nothing like I thought it would, and there have been moments when it has felt like I was just alone in the dark. I'm sharing this because, truth be told, we are all on our way home and I think all of us have moments when the road isn't quite what we thought it would be. I want to tell you that you are not alone in the dark. I am a mess but I know a Redeemer who chooses to use messes for His glory. If you've never seen His hands at work, I can tell you where to look. So often they are holding you in those moments when you thought you were alone in the dark.

Just as Hannah was forced to rely upon her car's GPS, we also need to know how to recognize the voice of our God's Positioning System (our GPS) in order to find our way during times of darkness. Listening to His voice will not only keep us going in the right direction, but it will allow us to have a constant "buddy" who will guide us and keep us safe from the attacks of unfriendlies. Listen closely, Dear Reader. His voice is clear and strong and loving, and He longs for you to know Him, hear Him, and follow Him into the security of that love.

You will pull me out of the net which they have secretly laid for me, For You are my strength. (Psalm 31:4)

Trail Notes:

Has there been a time in your life when you have faced lies from Satan? Explain.

If you decided to stray from God's path at that time, can you recognize why you chose to, and what (if any) consequences came from your decision?

If you chose to stay on God's path and not follow the temptation, what led you to that decision?

What can you do to tune into God's voice more clearly so that you can recognize Satan's tactics and you can choose to turn from them?

16

Too Close to the Edge - Temptations

No temptation has overtaken you except what is common to mankind. And God is faithful; He will not let you be tempted beyond what you can bear. But when you are tempted, He will also provide a way out so that you can endure it. I Corinthians 10:13 [27]

The best views I have experienced in my life have been from a mountain edge. The image is breathtaking. When I am standing on the edge of the cliff, I feel full of adrenaline and exhilaration. But there is an element of fear as well that didn't always exist for me. Looking over the edge to the steep plummet comes with a measure of hesitation and caution. When did I lose my nerve? When did I begin to see the danger in the high?

When I look at my children exploring the edge, I see their fearlessness. They love to push the limits, to get as close as they can to the edge, to see the fullness of the view and do whatever it takes to get the perfect shot. And I remember the day when I was fearless as well. Yet my fearlessness is no longer there. Now I approach the edge with concern for the safety of those in my care. I holler words of caution to my children as they run haphazardly toward the precipice. My heart drops every time they step too close. I believe this restraint has surfaced from two conditions: reality and experience. Reality shows me that we are not invincible and that some things actually are bigger than us. Experience reminds me that when we stand too close to the edge, bad things can happen, and we cannot predict the outcome when we act haphazardly.

I keep my children a safe distance from the edge to protect them from harm. I stand close to them and remind them often to pay attention to where they are walking. I urge them to remain constantly aware of their surroundings and footing. I encourage them to enjoy the view from the security of solid ground. I love them and long to keep them safe, despite their protests and desires to push the limits of the edge. Just as our Father does for us. He sees our faces when we set eyes on those spectacular views and knows our desire for the thrill; because of this He longs to pull us back and keep us safe. He cautions us against standing too close to the edge, as He knows full well the possible outcomes when we act haphazardly. It is our job to listen to His voice of reality and experience and trust it to protect us.

There will inevitably be times in your life when you are faced with situations that are risky and dangerous. It may be deciding whether to take a drink, partake in drugs, follow the wrong person home for the night, listen to bad advice, choose a toxic friend, cheat at work or school, click on that image on the screen, or many other choices that have the potential to have detrimental effects on our lives. These types of temptations could easily be equated with coming face to face with the edge of a steep cliff: The views may seem spectacular, but dancing too close to the edge can cause a catastrophic tumble.

We have all seen the movie or TV story line when an innocent actor is happily hiking along a path, sees a great view, continues to move toward the edge, loses his or her footing, and is sent sliding, tumbling, and rolling down the cliff. As adolescents and adults, we may find ourselves in a similar place. We are happily hiking along our path, when we are suddenly standing at a daunting precipice. We feel our footing is unsure. Sometimes we continue on in full confidence of our ability to navigate the treacherous path. Other times we question every step, knowing that one wrong move could plunge us over the edge. Either way, we are placing ourselves in a situation that may leave us literally hanging on for our lives.

I have stood on the edge of that figurative cliff. As with many young people, my college years brought with them a time of meeting new people and all the excitement that comes with new relationships. Unfortunately, this also brought with it a time when I wasn't making the best decisions for my life. As a Christian, I knew better than to push my relationships beyond a certain point, but as a young adult, I allowed fleshly desires to control where I was stepping. I made foolish choices. In the worldly sense my choices were acceptable. Yet in my Christian journey, those choices caused me to lose my footing and fall down a rock face that took me years to climb back up.

Remember that our measure for how close we can get to the edge is not the same as the world's. The world told me that there was nothing wrong with satisfying fleshly desires. It encouraged it, actually, by promising great views and a killer shot. Yet what the world failed to warn me of was the spiritual and emotional rocks and craggles that I would have to claw my way through in order to set myself back onto solid ground. The world promised the thrill, without care or concern for the consequence of the fall.

When we are faced with high risk situations, it takes both emotional and spiritual maturity to recognize the danger and to remain several steps away from the edge. When we are talking about life-altering situations, it is not a sign of weakness to step onto safer ground, but rather a sign of strength. The only sure way to avoid the fall is to avoid the edge. For some, the first taste can lead to addiction, the toxic relationship to emotional ruin, the wrong decision to a career suicide. We need to resolve now to keep ourselves away from those things that prove dangerous in our own lives.

Risky Business

We are constantly bombarded with risky temptations. The world will tell us that they are not really so risky. Friends and coworkers will assure us that there is no real danger and encourage us to step closer for a better view. When we begin to listen to the lies of the world, we gain a false sense of security in our footing. We become desensitized to the threat of sin. We fail to see the disaster that can come with one wrong move. Vic Redding writes about what happens when we stoop to the level of the world, in *Avoiding Satan's Snares:*

> *Romans 12:21 "Be not overcome of evil, but overcome evil with good." This world is overcome with evil and things of Satan.*

People don't blush anymore – even Christians. TV shows are getting worse and worse. Violence is over-taking streets and neighborhoods. Fornication and adultery are accepted as normal. Drug and alcohol abuse are destroying lives and families daily. We have got to stick to the standards in the word of God. In order to avoid stooping as Christians, we must refuse to do the things that the world accepts as normal.[28]

It is listening to the whispers of the world that cause us to veer from our path in Christ. Yet Christ's way is where we find safety and security. When we step away from His path, we expose ourselves to unforeseen dangers. While the world is whispering, Jesus is hollering words of caution to us. His Word is full of love and concern. Staying in obedience to Him allows us to find assurance in our direction and footing. "It is God who arms me with strength and keeps my way secure" (2 Samuel 22:33 NIV).

I realize how hard it is to make those crucial choices when faced with temptation. Our sinful nature of the flesh makes that view from the edge look awfully appealing. But we have to remind ourselves over and over that the view is not worth the risk. God has many magnificent sights planned for you in your journey. Let Him take you to them in the protection of His path. Just as I have no desire to rob my children of a great view from the mountaintop, neither does God want to rob of us of the same. He provides a way for us to enjoy the splendor of the sights while keeping us at a safe distance from danger. We are wise to heed the warnings of the One who cares for us. Pray for His strength to avoid temptation. He freely gives it. Remember, we cannot slip if we are not standing near the edge. Keep your distance, Young Traveler, it is much safer there.

Travel Notes:

Have you ever found yourself on the edge of risky behavior? If so, what was it and what was the inherent danger associated with it?

If you chose to act on the risk, did you suffer negative consequences for your decision? Think not just about worldly consequences such as getting caught or punished, but also relational and spiritual consequences. Describe them.

What did the world have to say about this behavior?

What protections can you put into place to keep yourself from walking too close to the edge of the world's temptations?

17

Financial Pitfalls - Finances

Keep your lives free of the love of money, and be content with what you have, because God has said "Never will I leave you; never will I forsake you." Hebrews 13:5[29]

Let me begin this section with a little author confession: I hate talking about finances. Do you know how we discussed what is in our personal gifts and talents backpack? Well, money management is most definitely *not* in mine. And to further my confession, this section was never one I intended on writing. However, during months of discussing challenges that young adults have faced and continue to face today, money management has appeared repeatedly across every generation. Therefore, I have swallowed my self-admitted deficiency and have brought to you the best of the knowledge that has been bestowed upon me by those much wiser than myself, in hopes that you will find it beneficial as well.

Unlike myself, the Bible is full of wisdom about finances. It seems as if it has been a hot topic for thousands of years. The Bible itself references money over 800 times. No wonder it is so overwhelming for us. Based on this, do you think that God sees money as an important topic as well? I believe that God mostly realizes that possessions and wealth are a challenge for His people. So much sin is rooted in people's desire for and misuse of money.

> For the love of money is the root of all kind of evil. Some people, eager for money, have wandered from the faith and pierced themselves with many griefs. (1 Timothy 6:10)

All one has to do is look around to see the multitude of people who have fallen into the pits of desperation due to money. Whether we stumble on that fat root of sin or wander off of God's path in search of worldly promises, we need to keep a keen eye out for financial pitfalls. They can be deep and wide, and ultimately they can swallow us up.

Throughout the Bible, we are told not to put our hopes in wealth and riches, but only in God. The New Testament advises, "Command those who are rich in this present world not to be arrogant nor to put their hope in wealth, which is so uncertain, but to put their hope in God, who richly provides us with everything for our enjoyment" (1

Timothy 6:17). Placing too much importance on wealth or equating possessions with happiness is so very dangerous for us.

I can tell you honestly that my husband and I live a frugal and simple life. Our careers have never afforded us great wealth, but we have been thankful and blessed abundantly because of that. Although we may not have vast knowledge of how to handle large amounts of money, we have always felt that we have gained much more wisdom and appreciation in how to handle what God has given to us. It has taken big faith, hard work, and large amounts of creativity to care for our family. I would not change these experiences for all the riches in the world. I tell you this to encourage you that you do not need large sums of money to find success in this world. Money will not buy happiness, love, or faith. These things are priceless and can be gained, no matter the size of your bank account. I know this sounds cliche, but I am living proof that it is true. For the believer, we do not need to place the state of our well-being on the state of our finances. Having the means to provide comfort for yourself and your family is critical, and we will discuss some tips on how to do this, but it is not required. God has to be enough.

It is important that we grasp this concept clearly. God does not intend for money to fulfill our needs. He demands that He alone is our Provider, whether He has chosen to bless us with financial abundance or not. He repeats often how He feels about us desiring money in search of security:

> *Whoever loves money never has enough; whoever loves wealth is never satisfied with their income. This too is meaningless. (Ecclesiastes 5:10)*

> *Better the little that the righteous have than the wealth of many wicked; for the power of the wicked be broken, but the LORD*

upholds the righteous. (Psalm 37:15-16)

God is clear that our reliance needs to be on Him, and He will provide for all of our needs. "No one can serve two masters. Either you will hate one and love the other, or you will be devoted to one and despise the other. You cannot serve both God and money" (Matthew 6:24). My prayer for you is that you keep these thoughts in mind as you begin your adult journey. Beyond any guidance I can provide below, let this be the one piece that you tuck away in your heart.

What's In Your Wallet?

Now that we have addressed the heart, let's address the wallet. Here are some basic tips that will get you started on your financial way. I encourage you to seek out more information on each of these points. The world of financial advice is vast and overwhelming, but there are many good Christian resources out there to be found. Never allow ignorance to be the cause of your demise. When it comes to finances, knowledge is power!

1. **Find your passion and your purpose**. You are about to or you have already begun your adult life. Hopefully, you have found your footing in being a child of Christ and you are working toward discovering what you have to offer the world. This discovery will come through much prayer, thought, and time. Work on finding out what passions God instilled in you and what His purpose is for you. I cannot stress enough the importance of remaining on His path at this time. Only then can we find confidence in what He has called us to do.

2. **Get out there!** You cannot discover where your path is leading if you don't take the necessary steps. You must start walking, trusting that God is leading you. You have your backpack on, your necessary tools in hand, and you now must do the leg work. Your career or life calling will not come knocking on your door.

You must hit the trail and move! Whether this be in the form of a formal education, internship, apprenticeship, job shadowing, job hunting, or mission work, never stop making forward progress toward finding your passion and purpose. Passion, purpose, progress. These things must fall in succession. You cannot have one without the other.

3. **Don't try to catch a free ride**. Money may go easily, but it does not come easily. Earning a living is hard work - always. There is no free ride through life. Despite what it may look like, there are no shortcuts or an easy buck. It is important to understand the value of money, and appreciate where it comes from. If someone chooses to employ you, they are valuing you enough to reward you with their hard-earned money. Never believe that you are doing someone a favor by taking their money. In turn, show gratitude and respect by working hard for each dollar you earn. A respectful attitude towards money will take you much further than the free ride promised by those trying to get rich quick.

4. **Seek Godly and wise counsel**. As stated earlier, there are many valid resources available for financial guidance. There are books, apps, audios, and programs that you can access that are specifically designed to provide a Christian perspective to financial planning. It is important that you seek a reliable source for hands-on guidance as well. Just as we spoke about finding a Sherpa mentor to help us through life, a financial mentor is also beneficial. One of the main reasons that people become afraid of money is because they are uneducated about it. Knowledge will empower you to take hold of your finances with confidence.

5. **Set yourself on the right track**. The number one tool that I have found beneficial in financial planning is setting up a budget. Just as a train that is on the right track can travel effortlessly to its destination, so can you if you lay the track for your finances. Let us look at a practical way of doing this:

Track Your Spending - Find out where your money is going. For a couple of months, track every dollar you spend so that you can gain an understanding of where each dollar is spent.

Set a budget - Once you know where your money is going, you can begin to tell it where it should go. Set a monthly budget and stick to it! By doing so, you get to tell your money what to do instead of it telling you what to do. There are multitudes of budgeting apps and programs to help you with this.

Spend only your income - There is a misconception out there that you have the ability to spend more money than you make. God has much to say about getting ourselves into debt: "The rich rules over the poor, and the borrower is the slave of the lender" (Proverbs 22:7). It is not wise, nor Biblical, to fall into debt. This is a practice that should be avoided at all costs. There is pride and confidence that comes when we are able to support ourselves without being indebted to another.

Tithe - God is clear about this. He requires that we give a portion of our income to Him. Jayson D. Bradley explains why:

> *Despite the fact that many people use the word "tithe" synonymously with any church-related giving, the word tithe literally means 'tenth.' The tithe was an obligatory offering from the law of Moses requiring 10 percent of an Israelite's first fruits. Because God provided the harvest, this first part was returned to him. It was a reminder to Israel that all things we have are his. It was a show of thankfulness for his provision. God intended to teach Israel about his sovereign ownership of everything. Instead of being consumers of their blessings, they had to stop and think through just how much blessing they had...Through the tithe, God took care of his people—and through the act of generous giving, God continues to bless his people.*[30]

Save up for a rainy day. One common piece of advice that I encountered in every article I read was that it is necessary that we save a portion of our money. God encourages us to do this as well: "The wise store up choice food and olive oil, but fools gulp theirs down" (Proverbs 21:20), and "The plans of the diligent lead to profit as surely as haste leads to poverty" (Proverbs 21:5). A general rule of thumb is to tuck away 10-15% of your earnings into savings whenever possible.

Ditch the credit cards! I am positive that among the tools that God packs for us for our journey, a credit card is not one of them. On the contrary, credit cards are like putting a rock into your backpack. Every time you become further in debt, you add more rocks. Before long, you are so weighed down by the financial burdens that you feel helpless and desperate; you may even feel unable to continue down the trail. There is a reason God warns of this; there is nothing more defeating than finding yourself in a financial crises due to debt. Do not fall prey to the promises of shiny rocks. Despite how pretty they look, they all weigh the same.

Put on your blinders. In an age of social media madness, it is hard to avoid the distractions of status symbols. It is important to understand what social media does to our psyche and how to combat its effect. Remember that when you are viewing others' lives, you are in essence seeing their very best. From our side of the screen, we all get to choose what we want others to see about us. Do not fall into a trap of comparing your blooper reel to someone else's motion picture. In other words, do not compare your real life status to their social media one. When you fail to recognize the difference, discontentment sets in and can lead to poor financial decisions.

One of the most toxic attitudes that we can possess is that of discontentment. We have addressed this in other areas throughout our journey, but it is possible that our desire for material possessions has the greatest ability to allow unhappiness to fester. When we allow our lives to be driven by our own desires we will mess up and miss what God has in store for us. In my opinion, finances may be one of the hardest parts of our lives to completely surrender to God. Not having control is very scary and unsettling. The irony is that no matter how hard we try we will never have complete control over what is God's to begin with.

I heard a radio sermon many years ago that spoke about stewardship. Do you know what the word *stewardship* means? It means manager. The Bible tells us that we are simply stewards of what God gives us, for everything is His. "The earth and everything in it, the world and its inhabitants, belong to the Lord" (Psalm 24:1). Art Rainer writes, "God owns everything, and we get to manage it for Him. The responsible management of these God-given resources is called stewardship."[31]

If someone were to hand you a stack of money and ask you to manage it for them, what would you do with that money? Would you go out and spend it frivolously? Would you invest it foolishly? Would you spend more than the person gave you and accumulate debt in their name as a result? It is vital that we view our finances as God's, so that we in turn make choices that honor Him.

Having an attitude of true stewardship will allow us to be thankful for what He has entrusted to us instead of being discontent with what He has not. Coming to a place of true surrender allows freedom for God to bless us in His full sovereignty and love. Will you choose to be content today? There is no better way to avoid landing face-first in a pit of discontentment than by finding joy in the abundance of God's provision.

Trail Notes:

How would you describe your financial status at this time? How do you feel about it?

What fears do you have about money or finances?

Is there any area of your finances that you feel you can improve upon?

Are you in a state of content or discontent about what God has chosen to give you at this time? What can you do to seek contentment today?

18

Slippery Slope - Mental Health

...do not fear, for I am with you, do not be afraid, for I am your God; I will strengthen you, I will help you, I will uphold you with my victorious right hand. Isaiah 43: 1-2

There is no doubt that one issue that has been seen among more and more young people is mental health. This phrase tends to carry with it negative connotations, and unfortunately, has been taboo in our culture for decades. I say *unfortunately* because it is a topic that holds no shame and needs to be discussed more openly among all generations. So let's kick this door wide open and be real with each other, ok?

I can almost bet that every person at least once in their lifetime has struggled with some form of mental or emotional problems. It may have come in the form of anxiety, stress, depression, post-traumatic stress disorder, grief, gender identity, or fear. We are all thinking, feeling individuals who are wading through a multitude of emotions each day. These emotions are influenced by other people, life events, hormones, brain chemicals, physical health, and many other factors. It would be preposterous to believe that any of us could go through life without ever having one or several of these things to send us sliding uncontrollably down a slippery slope of mental or emotional stress. Yet for some reason, although we have no problem telling other people about our physical ailments, we hesitate to tell them about our mental or emotional ones.

I am here to tell you that there is absolutely nothing wrong with us when we are battling a mental demon. And that is what it is - a battle. As stated before, Satan is very interested in gaining a foothold in our life. He desires to take our joy and fill us with despair. One of his most effective tools for this is to attack us at the core, and there is nothing closer to us than our own thoughts and feelings.

"Wait a minute!" you may be thinking, "Shawna, you aren't saying that I am filled with Satan if I am working through a mental or emotional issue, are you?" Absolutely not! What I am saying is that Satan will use mental health as a powerful tool over us, just as he uses desires of the flesh or greed or guilt against us. They are tools. Even those of us who have accepted Jesus as Lord of our life and are saved by His grace will spend our lives fighting off the advances of Satan. He has an arsenal full of weapons he will use to put a chink in our armor of faith. And I firmly believe that mental health is one of his weapons of mass destruction.

Dear Reader, the state of our mental and emotional health is key to how we make decisions, relate to others, and view our life. I have a pair of sunglasses that I love. The lenses have just the right tint to make everything look more colorful and vibrant. The only time I do not like to wear these particular glasses, however, is in autumn. When the leaves are turning their beautiful colors, my glasses make everything look absolutely stunning as the colors of the leaves come to life. Unfortunately, though, when I have to take the glasses off, I am always sorely disappointed in the reality of what I see around me. My vibrant oranges and reds become lack-luster browns and pinks. The world just seems dull.

Life can do this to us. There are times when the colors of our life become dulled. We are forced to take off the glasses that have colored life with vibrance and beauty and we must deal with the reality of pain and despair. It can cause us to feel disappointed, deflated, and defeated. Emotional and mental stress can cause this change of perspective. I want to encourage you that there is hope in sliding those shades back on and rediscovering the beauty and splendor that surrounds us. However, you will most likely not be able to do this alone.

Secure a Lifeline

The most predictable aspect of a slippery slope is that you cannot get back up that slope on your own accord. You most likely need someone or something to grab a hold of, to help to pull you up and onto dry ground. The same holds true to mental health. When we find ourselves sliding down that slope of distress, we need to immediately reach out for help. The longer we wait, the further we slide into despair and the harder it is to pull ourselves back up.

Imagine yourself sliding down a muddy slope. As you get further down the hill, you pick up speed, making it more and more difficult to find something to grab hold of. Now, if you knew there was someone or something at the top of the slope to help you from falling further, wouldn't you try with all of your might to grab onto it? You would stretch and lunge toward it in a desperate attempt to keep from sliding.

Similarly, when we feel ourselves sliding down the slope of mental or emotional despair, we need to muster every bit of energy we have to lunge toward what or who we know will bring us up safely. Our lifelines come in many forms: friends, family, mental health or medical professionals, pastoral or Christian counselors, and most importantly, Jesus. We need to not just reach out to them, we need to throw ourselves toward them as if our life depends on it. When our minds or emotions are in trouble, we risk everything. It is crucial that we seek help immediately. Do not wait until you have slipped too far. However, if you already have, do not be dismayed. There is always hope to find what will pull you up. Seek help now and pull with all of your might!

Anchor Yourself

Our slopes will come. Acknowledging their presence and preparing ourselves for them is a critical way to avoid the detriment of this trail hazard. We have one constant and reliable source of assistance in our lives, and that is Christ Himself. We need to set Him as our anchor, so that when we begin to slide, we already have a lifeline in place. He stands firm and pulls us back to Him. Every time. And when we do find ourselves slipping, we need to reach out immediately and unashamedly and without fear.

Suffering in this life is inevitable. We are broken people and incapable from birth of properly coping with the effects of the world's sin. Therefore, there is not one person immune from the grip of mental or emotional distress. One reason that our sights are dulled is to point us to our need for the brilliance of Jesus. Without our suffering and recognition of our insufficiency, we would fail to realize the importance of His redemption.

Do you remember my glasses? The beauty of Christ is that He colors our lives just as my glasses do. When we do not have Jesus, the events in our lives that dull our world can leave us feeling hopeless, as if we will never see its brilliance again. A young friend of mine describes this phenomenon perfectly:

> *How we* feel *doesn't reflect the reality of Christ. Even though we may not feel like God is with us in the same way when we're dealing with mental health, He actually is, and remembering that our feelings or 'vision' don't reflect accurately the truth about reality is a powerful weapon in dealing with it.*

Yet through Jesus, we find the hope to see His glory! We see our lives through *His* lenses, and only then can we rest our minds in His redeeming grace and love.

Frailty Doesn't Equal Failure

As I was preparing for this chapter there was an idea in my heart, yet I could not verbalize it. I took it to the Lord and prayed to Him to direct me and send me some inspiration. Feeling frustrated, I opened Facebook for some needed distraction. By the second post on my screen God had answered my prayer. There on the page was a quote by Lysa Terkheurst, "Just because you are struggling doesn't mean you are failing." As He has proven over and over to me, God sent me exactly what my heart wanted to write, but my mind could not comprehend. Praise be to Him for His constant provision and desire to thrill us!

Friends, I have spent my life among people, young and old and myself included, who have convinced themselves that moments of frailty in life mean that they are failing in life. A teen tossed about by turbulent emotions. A young adult questioning why she hasn't married. A groom anxious about providing for his new bride. A mom insecure in her child-rearing abilities. A father depressed from a job loss. The scenarios could go on forever. The bottom line is that there are numerous situations that leave us vulnerable to attacks of self-doubt.

This is where the danger lies - when we begin to slide and refuse to reach out for help; when we attempt to handle our emotional and mental problems on our own. This typically results from us feeling that reaching out for help is a sign of weakness, that we are raising the white flag of surrender to our frailty. On the contrary, the only weakness is found when we fail to admit that we need help. Do not fall prey to the idea that when we struggle with life issues we are actually failing to handle them. This could not be farther from the truth. It is in our ability to reach out and admit our frailty that we find the strength to regain our footing as we slip and slide downhill.

I would consider myself a neat freak. Well, at one time I did. My first year of homeschooling, my children were ages 1, 3, and 5, one being a child with special needs. Each day as my younger two were napping, my kindergartner would sit quietly at his desk by the window and ask in his sweet voice, "when are we doing school today?" He loves learning and even then looked forward to the time with Mom.

Day after day, he sat and waited while I frantically scurried around trying to clean my house from the tornadoes that swirled around young children. I could not focus on teaching him while my house was in disarray. So he waited, and I cleaned. Consequently, I felt like a complete failure. I was not able to hold all that life was handing me. I was full of anxiety and on the verge of a mental breakdown.

I distinctly remember one afternoon, sitting under my oak tree with my children playing in the yard, that I called out to God in complete desperation. I could not do it all. I was broken in my inability. I asked God that very day to take something from me. I knew that I could not continue to teach my children and be the mom I needed to be with my obsessive tendencies. I asked Him to strip me of the focus on my home and allow me to focus on my family. Boy, did I wonder later at the wisdom in this request!

From that moment on, the clutter and the dust and the material chaos seemed insignificant to me. Okay, I will admit that it does annoy me from time to time, especially when it becomes out of control, but for the most part I am able to overlook what I never could have before. My husband could possibly tell you that this has a blessing and a curse, for although this means that my house will never grace the pages of *Better Homes and Gardens,* it does mean that I am in a much healthier mental and emotional state, and therefore a much better mother and wife. Since that very day, God has lifted that anxiety from me and replaced it with pure acceptance of my domestic shortcomings.

It was critical that I sought help at this time in my life. I was at my breaking point. I bore the weight of guilt and shame of my inability to be everything to everyone. In reality, it was a weight much greater than I was able to carry, and honestly, I should have sought help sooner. How thankful I am for a gracious God who heard the cries of His hurting child and so lovingly and willing pulled her up, muddy and tattered, from the slippery slope of depression.

Frailty does not equal failure.

Trials will come and events will happen that are too much for us to bear.

The secret is that God doesn't intend for us to be able to.

When we attempt to independently claw our way up from those pits of despair, we put blinders on to acknowledging our limitations. It is in the acceptance of our weaknesses that the blinders are removed and we clearly see our need for Him. Only then can we gain the strength we need to reach dry ground.

Do not be fooled, Dear One. If you are struggling, you are far from failing. You are just that - struggling. Take a moment to acknowledge where you are feeling weak, ask God to show you what you can learn in this moment of weakness, and then trust in His provision of the needed assistance to find your way to safety.

God is faithful to show us the way; however, we have the responsibility to reach out and to accept the help He provides. Finding emotional and mental health takes courageous acts of faith, yet it is in each step of faith that we build the spiritual muscles to get us safely through our next challenge.

Travel Notes:

Have you in the past or are you currently experiencing any emotional or mental stress?

What areas of your life are contributing to this?

Although we know that Jesus is our anchor in times of mental or emotional stress, who else can you turn to in order to get help when you feel you are slipping down a slope of negative mental health?

VI

Are You Ready?

19

Adventure Awaits - Next Steps

No eye has seen, no ear has heard, no mind has imagined the things that God has prepared for those who love him. I Corinthians 2:9[32]

We've spent the past eighteen chapters digging into many aspects of this amazing journey that encompasses all of the elements of your life. You are at an incredible time in your life. You are ending one phase and you are hopefully geared up and ready to begin the adventure of this new one! For parents, this is a time of letting go. For young adults, this is a time of heading out. Either way, it is bound to be full of hills and valleys, cliffs and boulders, and the most amazing sights you could ever imagine.

You are looking toward the summit and my prayer is that you understand that the only way that we can reach this magnificent place is by accepting the Son that God sent us to lead us there. Our acceptance of Jesus as our Guide Rope ensures our safety as we tackle every element that we will encounter. Once we clip into Him, we find security despite the inclement weather, dangerous terrain, and seemingly insurmountable obstacles in our path. Along with this, God has provided us a detailed Trail Guide full of wisdom, direction, encouragement, and guidelines to show us what to do in every twist and turn of our path. Hopefully you have realized all of the resources that God has blessed you with for your individual path and you are feeling ready to shoulder your pack, confident that it will provide you with every necessary tool.

It is now that you are standing at the trail head, anxious for what lies ahead, secure in your preparation, and ready to take your first steps into adulthood. Parents, it is at this same trail head that we rest in confidence of who our children have become and how readily equipped they are in Christ.

Young Person, your path will not always be smooth, and your footing may falter at times, but finding strength in who you were made to be and in Who made you will ensure a rewarding adventure! Remember that a regular assessment of your environment will help you to make necessary adjustments so that you can not only survive, but grow and thrive. In that, it is essential to surround yourself with a community of believers who are there to support and encourage you in challenging times in your life.

Even more so, it is vital to have traveling partners to share in your journey. A wise friend once told me that we all need someone to walk ahead of us to guide us, someone to walk beside us to share life's experiences, and someone behind us to follow in our footsteps. This is where you will find the importance of having a mentor, but also of being a mentor. Your purpose on this earth is to lead others to Christ. You will have times in your life when you can do nothing but focus on the footprints ahead of you, but at some point you must realize your position of importance in helping another hiker reach their summit. Do not underestimate how much God longs for you to be a Sherpa for His kingdom trek. You are valuable to the Kingdom, Friend. Never forget that.

Along with mentors and Christian companions, your path may intersect with a spouse, who comes equipped with a pack full of resources to benefit your joint excursion. This is when you may gain clarity of your own gifts and talents and see in full God's design for them. However, if God chooses not to intersect your path with another in marriage, rest in confidence that He has mighty work planned for your life as a single traveler. Regardless of your relationship status, God is going to do amazing things through you!

Whether defined by your career, family make-up, ministry, education, or community, when you are tuned into God, He will fill you with a passion, unfold His purpose for that passion, and set you on the right path to make progress toward fulfilling His will for your life. You will do great deeds for Christ, Dear Reader! Place your trust in Him and allow Him to direct your steps. There is no greater satisfaction than to know that your life is directly aligned with His will. The world and Satan will throw every trail hazard at you to prevent this, but do not be fooled - you are perfectly suited to accomplish all that God has intended for you. Believe it. Live it.

I am excited for you to take this next step. There may never be another time in your life that comes with more change, uncertainty, excitement, and promise. Early adulthood is a flurry of emotions stemming from the necessary separation from childhood and the enormity of stepping into the independence of adulthood. Do not be discouraged if you experience some moments that leave you breathless. There will be times along your journey when you will face hills to climb. You will grow tired and out of breath. That is a normal sensation. You will have to stop and catch your breath before you go on. But you rest, and then you begin to put one foot in front of the other again. Before you know it, the trail levels off and things begin to seem easier. There will even be times of downhill slopes or beautiful sights, when life is pleasant and scenic and refreshing. These are the times we cling to in thanksgiving for eyes to see the beauty and legs to carry us through.

Even the most seasoned adult finds himself turned around at times. Just remember to listen to the voice of the One who holds your coordinates. Your GPS is always at work, guiding, loving, leading, and working all things for good. "For I am sure of this, that He who began a good work in you will bring it to completion at the day of Jesus Christ" (Philippians 1:6).

Your journey has just begun. Oh, what glorious sights await you along the way! Grab your stick, gear up, and let's hit the trail.

Travel Notes:

Take a moment to assess your direction:
  What is your passion?

What purpose does God have for you to use this passion?

What steps will you take to make progress towards His purpose for you?

As you enter adulthood, what are some of the uncertainties you face? How do you see yourself overcoming them?

You are on a new adventure, what is your next step in your journey? What do you need to do to prepare yourself for the trail?

Notes

THE PATH - GOD'S PLAN

1   "Forest Path in Krkonose" by Roman Boed is licensed under CC BY 2.0

GETTING TO THE SUMMIT - ETERNAL DESTINATION

2   "Electric Peak from Bunsen Peak Summit" by Jacob W. Frank is licensed under Public Domain, CC

3   Shorter, Keith. "I Am the Way, Week 7." Mt. Airy Baptist Church, Easley. 16 August 2018. Sermon.

4   Barna Group. "What Millenials Want When They Visit Church." *Millenials and Generations.* 4 March 2015. Web. August 2018.

CLIPPING IN - FAITH IN ACTION

5   "Clipping In" by Justin Jensen is licensed under CC BY 2.0.

BACKPACKS - GIFTS AND TALENTS

6   "The Hike" by Alan Levine is in the Public Domain, CC0

ON YOUR OWN - ADULTHOOD

7   "Hiker" by Brandon Atkinson is licensed under CC BY 2.0

FINDING YOUR FOOTING - IDENTITY

8   Altrogge, Mark. "17 Powerful Bible Verses About the Future to Give You Peace." *God's Faithfulness.* 13 December 2012. Web. September 2018.

9   Hagin, Kennith W. "Our Identity in Christ." *Kennith Hagin Ministries.* September 2016. Web. September 2018.

SOIL ANALYSIS - ENVIRONMENT

10   "Bindweed plant breaking through asphalt 7 - P1030679" by Mark Dixon is licensed
        under CC BY 2.0

SEPARATION ANXIETY - FOR PARENTS

11 "Brown Rope Tangled and Formed Into Heart Shape on Brown Wooden Rail" is licensed under CC0

12 Ries, Brian. McKirdy, Euan. Whiteman, Hillary. Wagner, Meg. "All 12 Boys and Soccer Coach Rescued from Thai Cave." *CNN*. 10 July 2018. Web. August 2018.

13 Flood, Rob. "Children Need Praying Parents." *CRU*. 4 July 2016. Web. August 2018.

DIVING INTO THE CURRENT - COMMUNITY OF BELIEVERS

14 "River - 2" by Dave Collier is licensed under CC BY 2.0

SHERPAS - MENTORS

15 "Sherpa Porter" by smallufo is licensed under CC BY 2.0

16 Foreman, Bruce. "The Sherpa cheat sheet: 9 things you were embarrassed to ask." *CNN*. 12 July 2017. Web. September 2018.

17 "Guide: What Does a Sherpa at Mt. Everest Do?" *Newsround*. 23 April 2014. Web. September 2018.

18 http://www.everest1953.co.uk/how-important-are-sherpas-on-mount-everest

TRAVELING SOLO - SINGLENESS

19 "Satisfied Hiker Enjoying Breathtaking Views, Mount Whitney Summit, 14,505 Feet, California" by Ken Lund is licensed under CC BY 2.0

POINT OF CONVERGENCE - MARRIAGE

20 Photo credit: Caroline Batson

21 Masonheimer, Phylicia. "Why Being Unequally Yoked is More Dangerous than You Think." *Crosswalk.com*. 22 February 2017. Web. August 2018.

22 https://www.merriam-webster.com/dictionary/yoke

COMBINING RESOURCES - TEAMWORK

23 "Hikers in the Wilderness" by Bureau of Land Management is licensed under CC BY 2.0

24 https://en.wikipedia.org/wiki/Rope

A KAYAK IN THE DESERT - DIFFERENCES

25 "@The Desert Tortoise Natural Area" by jvoves is licensed under CC BY 2.0

THIEVES AND ROBBERS - SPIRITUAL ATTACKS

26 photo by pfly is licensed under CC BY-SA 3.0

TOO CLOSE TO THE EDGE - TEMPTATIONS

27   "Echo Mountain Hike" by Megan Rosenbloom is licensed under CC BY 2.0

28   http://faithfreewill.org/assets/avoiding-satan-s-snares.pdf

FINANCIAL PITFALLS - FINANCES

29   "Big Sur Mud Run 2011" by Presidio of Monterey is in the Public Domain

30   https://pushpay.com/blog/20-bible-verses-about-tithing/

31   Rainer, Art. "11 Awesome Stewardship Bible Verses." *Art Rainer*. 21 March 2016. Web. January 2019.

ADVENTURE AWAITS - NEXT STEPS

32   "One Step at a Time" by Jasen Miller is licensed under CC BY 2.0

About the Author

Shawna Talley (Barista Mama Ministries) can be found in Easley, South Carolina serving up a hot cup of Joe alongside solid advice and a listening ear. Her barstools are most often occupied by her husband, Chris, and their four children, but they are regularly joined by those who have figured out that the Barista Mama lives up to her name and spreads motherly love and wisdom to all who are near her. Shawna uses her bachelor of science from Clemson University by providing purposeful programming for audiences ranging from children to senior adults, where she passionately shares encouragement and God's Truths.

You can connect with me on:
🌐 https://shawnatalley.wordpress.com
f https://www.facebook.com/Barista-Mama

53016907R00117

Made in the USA
Columbia, SC
09 March 2019